The Analysis
of Policy Impact

The Analysis
of Policy Impact

Edited by
John G. Grumm
Wesleyan University

Stephen L. Wasby
State University of New York
  at Albany

LexingtonBooks
D.C. Heath and Company
Lexington, Massachusetts
Toronto

Library of Congress Cataloging in Publication Data

Main entry under title:
  The Analysis of policy impact.

  1. Policy sciences—Addresses, essays, lectures. I. Grumm, John G.
II. Wasby, Stephen L., 1937-
H61.A657   361.6'1   80-8636
ISBN 0-669-03951-9

Published simultaneously in Canada

Printed in the United States of America

International Standard Book Number: 0-669-03951-9

Library of Congress Catalog Card Number: 80-8636

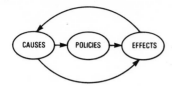

Policy Studies Organization Series

Specific Policy Problems

Analyzing Poverty Policy
    edited by Dorothy Buckton James
Crime and Criminal Justice
    edited by John A. Gardiner and Michael Mulkey
Civil Liberties
    edited by Stephen L. Wasby
Foreign Policy Analysis
    edited by Richard L. Merritt
Economic Regulatory Policies
    edited by James E. Anderson
Political Science and School Politics
    edited by Samuel K. Gove and Frederick M. Wirt
Science and Technology Policy
    edited by Joseph Haberer
Population Policy Analysis
    edited by Michael E. Kraft and Mark Schneider
The New Politics of Food
    edited by Don F. Hadwiger and William P. Browne
New Dimensions to Energy Policy
    edited by Robert Lawrence
Race, Sex, and Policy Problems
    edited by Marian Lief Palley and Michael Preston
American Security Policy and Policy-Making
    edited by Robert Harkavy and Edward Kolodziej
Current Issues in Transportation Policy
    edited by Alan Altshuler
Security Policies of Developing Countries
    edited by Edward Kolodziej and Robert Harkavy
Determinants of Law-Enforcement Policies
    edited by Fred A. Meyer, Jr., and Ralph Baker
Evaluating Alternative Law-Enforcement Policies
    edited by Ralph Baker and Fred A. Meyer, Jr.
International Energy Policy
    edited by Robert M. Lawrence and Martin O. Heisler
Employment and Labor-Relations Policy
    edited by Charles Bulmer and John L. Carmichael, Jr.
Housing Policy for the 1980s
    edited by Rogert Montgomery and Dale Rogers Marshall
Environmental Policy Formation
    edited by Dean E. Mann
Environmental Policy Implementation
    edited by Dean E. Mann
The Analysis of Judicial Reform
    edited by Philip L. Dubois
The Politics of Judicial Reform
    edited by Philip L. Dubois
Critical Issues in Health Policy
    edited by Ralph Straetz, Marvin Lieberman, and Alice Sardell

Contents

Preface

Until recently, policy analysis has been marked by a division of labor among social scientists. Political scientists have devoted themselves to the study of policy making, or the process by which "inputs" are turned into "outputs." Other social scientists then have sought to determine the consequences of these outputs for society, the economy, or U.S. relations abroad. Economists, for example, have applied their analytical tools to the question of how various fiscal policies have affected or are likely to affect inflation, unemployment, the interest rate, and many other aspects of the economic system. We would not expect them to be, and they have not been, particularly concerned with the details of how that policy emerged from the legislative process.

Five years ago one of us (Grumm 1975) noted that relatively little research had been completed by political scientists on the analysis of policy impact. This no longer is the case. The change became particularly evident to us as we considered the vast number of proposals for chapters to appear in this book. Political scientists in great numbers have joined their fellow social scientists and other investigators in seeking answers to the intriguing question: What factors in the policy-making process itself, in the content of the policy, or in the manner it was implemented were responsible for the actual consequence of the policy?

We continue to owe a debt to Harold Lasswell, who told us some years ago that the impact of public policies on individuals and groups is as much a political datum as is the impact of individuals and groups on public policies (Lasswell 1951), and to David Easton, who reminded us that the political process does not end at the output stage but continues as the outputs affect the environment of the political system and, in turn, produce new inputs (Easton 1965). Along with a growing acceptance of Lasswell's notion that a policy orientation is a central concern of political science has come the realization that such an orientation implies treating policy as an independent as well as a dependent variable, as a cause as well as a consequence.

Despite the expansion of policy-impact research by political scientists and others, there has been a regrettable lack of theoretical development in the field. The reason, partly, is that most policy-impact studies have been motivated by practical considerations; there has been a need to find answers to pressing questions. To the extent that such research is useful, it certainly is not to be deplored, but eventually we must come to terms with the realization that we are producing not a cumulative body of knowledge but only a mass of atomized findings. We, the editors and the authors of this book, have addressed this problem as best we could and trust that we have made some theoretical and empirical advances in the field. We have inevitably been limited by the state of the art at the present time, a state that we believe is well reflected in a review of the proposed chapters for this book, which shows a heavy reliance on the case-study approach. There is little comparative work either across substantive areas or across political boundaries. We have chosen to include in this book those studies that we believe had the greatest potential for making a theoretical contribution, though there is little here in the way of an overarching integrative or theory-developing work.

Another underlying problem that inhibits theoretical advancement is a methodological one. Conventionally, social and political analysis is directed toward finding explanations for some phenomenon in state or society. Many well-worn techniques can be used when public policy is the phenomenon to be explained—that is, when it is treated as the dependent variable. But such techniques are not necessarily appropriate in a research design where the tables are turned and we are given an explanation or a cause and then asked to find the effects. This is by no means an insurmountable problem, but it is one of which we need to be more aware. Much of the initial work by political scientists in analyzing policy impacts has been characterized by methodological confusion, and we can expect this to persist unless researchers in the field generally become more attentive to the appropriateness of their methodologies. We have tried to address this problem as well as we could but have found that awareness of this problem has not spread very far or wide. We are pleased, however, to be able to include three chapters that deal directly with important research needs and methods. Furthermore, several of the other chapters throughout the book show a keen awareness of methodological considerations.

Reading through and considering the many chapters and proposals for chapters for this book proved to be an informative experience. One of the most startling impressions was the central role that politics and government actors are said to have in the process by which policy does or does not have impacts. At times the authors make this explicit; at other times, they do not; but their intent, nevertheless, is clear from the focus of the studies. We say this is startling because of the controversy of some years back over the relative roles of socioeconomic factors and political factors in determining policy. Indeed, from our present vantage point, it is difficult to remember that those asserting the primacy of political variables had to strive mightily to "get back into the ballgame." Perhaps our focus on the impact of policy rather than on its development explains why socioeconomic factors are given relatively little attention in this book, but we still consider that the relative absence of attention is not obvious; certainly, if socioeconomic factors are held, by some, to be the major determinants of policy itself, they should also be thought to affect the impact of that same policy significantly.

We have also become aware that a disturbing gap exists between the efforts of students of the legal process, who concentrate on the impact of judicial decisions, and the work of those coming to policy analysis from a broader American government tradition or from training in public administration, who study the effects of legislative and administrative policy. Cross-fertilization between the two groups, desired for some time, remains a relatively vain hope or at least an unrealized one. The volume on civil liberties policy that one of us edited several years ago (Wasby 1976) contained much material of a constitutional law (doctrinal) genre, with little application of more sophisticated policy-analytic approaches and techniques then widely in use. This present book contains no studies in which policy-analytic techniques are applied to the important judicial decisions of the last twenty-five years or so. (However, those interested in civil rights are applying policy-analytic techniques to administrative-compliance problems in that field.)

We have grouped the articles in this book under five topics. In the first and longest part (six chapters), factors that may affect the impact of policies are presented. Through studies of law enforcement, human rights, black voter participation, antidiscrimination laws, and equal-employment opportunity, we see the role of intraorganizational and interorganizational variables, attitudinal variables affecting compliance, social differentiation, and symbolism as an intended impact of policy. In the next part, we use studies of federalism and urban problems to turn to unintended impacts of policies. The way in which policy impact may feed back into further development of policy is explored through studies of the environment (a not-uncommon subject for policy analysis), divorce law (far less commonly studied), and an attempt to "terminate" an Indian tribe. From this collection of studies in which the impact of substantive policy is the primary focus, we turn to two other topics. The first is the methodology of policy analysis, explored through an explication of analysis of policy on the family, a study incorporating and evaluating several linear-trend models in relation to reapportionment, and an examination of an impact-analysis project incorporated into an ongoing special-education program. The second is the role of social scientists in performing policy analysis. Here policy-analysis practitioners share their experiences that have led them to develop some principles of practice and some cautionary words and develop a set of roles for the effective policy analyst.

References

Easton, David. 1965. *A Framework for Political Analysis*. Englewood Cliffs, N.J.: Prentice-Hall.

Grumm, John G. 1975. "The Analysis of Policy Impact." In Fred I. Greenstein and Nelson W. Polsby, eds., *Handbook of Political Science*, vol. 6. Reading, Mass.: Addison-Wesley.

Lasswell, Harold D. 1951. "The Policy Orientation." In Daniel Lerner and
     Harold D. Lasswell, eds., *The Policy Sciences: Recent Developments in
     Scope and Method*. Stanford, Calif.: Stanford University Press.
Wasby, Stephen L., ed. 1976. *Civil Liberties Policy and Policy-Making*.
     Lexington, Mass.: Lexington Books, D.C. Heath and Co.

Part I
Factors Affecting
Policy Impact

The chapters in this part address a number of factors that affect the impact of policy, but they focus primarily on those factors integral to government itself. The first three chapters address various aspects of the bureaucratic side of policy impact. Marshall Carter, considering border policy, explores conflicting pressures that result in border management inconsistent with central national policy. She stresses such matters as interagency rivalries and conflicts over jurisdiction. Debra Stewart then directs our attention to administrative organizational practices with respect to equal-employment-opportunities policy, specifically the conditions under which particular organizational features have an impact and how they affect the intensity of impact. In a shift of focus, Harold Molineu stresses the need for us to look at the "impression of implementation" rather than merely at substantive changes. Using President Carter's human-rights policy, he points to domestic and symbolic consequences of foreign policy, particularly in terms of administrative alterations.

How the implementation of a law can result in public policy quite different from what the law's supporters intended is revealed in M. Margaret Conway's study of the Equal Credit Opportunity Act of 1974. She found the process of regulation drafting and the resulting content of the regulations to be important factors in accounting for this difference. As did Marshall Carter, she also discovered that implementation problems are vastly increased when a multitude of federal agencies is given responsibility for enforcement. Ronald Terchek's study of the Voting Rights Act of 1965 provides an example of very direct federal policy intervention. Still the impact of this intervention showed considerable variation. By constructing an index based on Robert Dahl's concept of polyarchy and relating this to black voting participation, he was able to account for much of this variation. Bringing this part to a close, Fred Coombs treats five major bases for noncompliance with policy: problems with communication, insufficient resources, objections to the goals of and assumptions underlying policy or to the actions required to reach those goals, and questions of authority on which the policy is based.

1 Policy Organization and Impact: Fragmentation in the Borderlands

Marshall Carter

Policy is a rather vague term, referring to a prudent or advantageous course of action, guiding principle, or procedure. It has, however, a second, less-dignified meaning: a form of gambling on unpredictable numbers. The latter usage is curiously appropriate for the purposes and actions associated with our borders as a nation-state.

Borders are among the most intractable and yet variable elements of the nation-state system, based as it is upon centralized control of territory (Starr and Most 1976). The presence of national boundaries is essentially a condition of statehood. The actuality of borders, however, depends upon a host of past events, present acts, and future intentions, some of which are conscious responses to contemporary conditions, while others are unconscious consequences of history. Within the nation-state, far from the border, various interests make demands that affect the border and its surrounding zone, the borderlands (contiguous areas daily and visibly influenced by the presence of the border and the neighboring state and society). Interests within the borderlands—either unique to this zone or simply regional variants of wider interests—struggle among themselves and also direct demands to the center. The central government bears the responsibility for the maintenance of the border and the contingent conditions of the borderlands. Policy making and implementation, however, is often shared, willingly or not, with others, and this complicates both action and analysis.

We have little theory to guide us in the analysis of borders—either particular borders or border matters generally—although there is much historical and contemporary material relating to borders upon which to draw (Fernandez 1977; Price 1971). Neither the study of political organization and behavior nor the field of comparative politics has much to say about the boundaries of the various political models offered, a curious phenomenon. The nation-state, which has been dominant in both theory

This chapter is based upon research in El Paso from 1976 through 1979, including interviews at all federal, state, and local agencies with border concerns, and interviews at the headquarters of the various federal agencies in Washington, D.C., in November and December 1978. I wish to thank the many informants whose assistance is reflected in this essay and also to note the editorial assistance of Stephen Wasby. The views found herein are my own and do not in any way represent those of the Foreign Service of the Department of State.

3

and practice, must certainly be defined, enclosed, demarcated. The form
and operation of its institutions of governing are widely studied in all their
variations. The form and operation of the boundaries can, and do, also
assume many different patterns, including patterns of relationships along
these boundaries, variations that have drawn relatively little attention.
Among the consequences is the rudimentary state of border-policy and implementation analysis (Zartman 1965).

Students of foreign policy and organizational behavior, two fields of
obvious applicability, have done little to explore border-policy issues.
Policy analysts have tended to define problems either cross-nationally or in-
tranationally, with binational and boundary affairs quite literally on the
periphery. Organizational studies provide case examinations of single agencies, often at a particular moment, rather than analyses of long-term
fragmentation and conflict among a group of agencies that develop and administer a policy. The more promising exceptions focus upon the policy
makers and administrators themselves and on their battles for personal and
policy advancement (Heclo 1977).

The most specialized subfield, the study of the foreign-policy apparatus, appears at first glance to be the most directly relevant to border
policy because affairs of borders are, by definition, matters of foreign-
relations concern. A rather substantial body of research and prescription in
this field developed as the international interests of the United States expanded in the postwar era. Even here, however, the thrust of the description
and analysis is turned away from the border. A large amount of the work
has gone into single-agency studies, primarily of the Department of State
(Campbell 1971; Esterline and Black 1975; Warwick et al. 1975). Another
substantial portion is concerned with the Washington apparatus and who
controls it; this tends to exclude both nontraditional foreign-policy agencies, such as the Department of Commerce and extrafederal agencies
(Allison and Szanton 1976; Bacchus 1974; Destler 1972; Halperin 1974;
Rourke 1973). These exclusions constitute a very large segment of the network that formulates and applies policy at the borders.

Border-policy analysis, however, can find material of use in the foreign-
policy and organization catalog, even if the particular topic under discussion is far removed from the border. McCormick and Kihl, for example,
have provided some stimulating suggestions in an analysis of intergovernmental organizations' impact on foreign-policy behavior; among such
organizations are many binational border agencies (1979, pp. 499-504). The
process of decision making on a foreign-policy issue, such as the Cuban
missile crisis, may bear even closer similarities to the process of decision
making on border questions. Graham Allison's study of the missile crisis,
which sets out three models of the process as a whole (1971, pp. 10-38,
67-100, 144-184), has laid the groundwork for an examination of the com-

plex interactions of individuals and agencies in other cases. It is unfortunate that little work has been undertaken with these models as a guide since Allison's initial study.

The brief notes on organization and action in the borderlands that follow are intended only to reopen this approach as far as policy and implementation of border affairs is concerned, focusing on the model of organizational process as the major factor in explaining a decision or an entire policy.

Policy and Machinery: The El Paso Case

Whatever the specifics of border policy and the extent of its rationality in Allison's terms, it must be implemented through administrative agencies, the nature of which affect policy itself. In the United States-Mexican case, these agencies are a complex and somewhat confused set, fragmented in three ways dysfunctional to ready implementation of a centrally determined intention. First, there are divisions between local and general (national) interests. These are closely related to, but not duplicates of, the rifts between the interests and perceptions of the borderlands as opposed to those of the heartlands, and perhaps even those of the state itself as a political entity. Third, there are multiple agencies at the center, which are often at odds with one another as organizations and whose battles reverberate along the border.

The El Paso sector offers a good view of these problems. As the largest urban site on the border, it is host to nearly all of the fractious federal agencies, as well as numerous local border-oriented private and public organizations (Bath 1978; Carter 1979). The changing pressures upon, and interests of, the federal government regarding the southwestern border have combined with the growth of El Paso and its sister city, Juárez (together containing over a million persons in 1979), to produce an administrative jumble. No single U.S. agency has, or has had, sole, major, or even coordinating authority on border and borderlands policy at the center. Federalism and the competitive nature of bureaucracies, combined with a series of not entirely consistent judicial opinions on immigration law and rights of aliens, have created a vast maze for the making and implementation of border policy, within which relationships and powers are indefinite and shifting.

On the border itself, the apparatus is smaller but equally labyrinthine. The primary agencies in the El Paso sector are those of the Immigration and Naturalization Service (INS), including the Border Patrol, under the Department of Justice; the Customs Service and its patrol under the Department of the Treasury; and offices of the Department of State, including a consulate in Juárez. Treasury also has local offices of the Bureau of Alcohol, Tobacco and Firearms (BATF) and the Secret Service. The Fish and Wildlife Service and the Parks Service of the Department of the Interior, the Public Health Service of the Department of Health and Human Services, and the Animal and Plant Health Inspection Service of the Department of Agriculture all have border responsibilities. Even the Federal Aviation Administration keeps an eye on the border. The military base at Fort Bliss may lend a hand to other agencies. And two relatively new agencies, the Drug Enforcement Administration (DEA) and the El Paso Intelligence Center (EPIC), have major border-control duties. EPIC was established by DEA in August 1974 and now operates jointly with INS, BATF, Customs, FAA, and the Coast Guard along the entire two-thousand-mile border. Its major goal is to gather all available data about the border that might be relevant to narcotics smuggling, pooling and disseminating information from federal agencies, and, since late 1977, granting access to all law-enforcement agencies. EPIC is thus of interest as the closest approximation to a command center for the border. Although its performance in this role is limited both by its specialization and by its function as a communications tool, it offers a possible model for interagency policy coordination.

Constitutionally there is no state or local authority over border policy or maintenace because this is a federal power. For example, arrests on suspicion of illegal entry are not, in theory, made by city or county police. However, numerous state and local government agencies have border concerns, a fact recognized by the federal government itself in the establishment of the Southwest Border Regional Commission. The state liquor-control board, the comptroller's office, narcotics agents, and other state police watch the border for their own purposes, and often they work without the presence or cooperation of federal authorities. Various Texas labor, education, health, welfare, and judicial authorities have adopted policies toward aliens that clash with those of the federal government and with those of neighboring states as well (Corwin 1978, pp. 67-68, 78-84, 165; Waddle 1977). Local authorities—police, housing, school boards—are active. Surrounding this official network is one of private interests: railroads, textile and clothing manufacturers, bonded warehouses and duty-free shops, commercial sales, labor unions, the Organization of U.S. Border Cities and Counties, the Catholic Conference, the League of United Latin American Citizens, and the United Fund. These groups have varying, often conflicting, preferences about the border. Some take action on their own; others are legally charged with a border role. Railroads, for example, are liable to fines for failure to prevent crossings on their international bridges.

The rational actor model posited by Allison (1971, pp. 10-38) does not seem to fit the border very well. It is far from self-evident that a clear, coherent federal border policy exists or is being formulated (Cornelius 1977; Garza and Cehelsky 1979; Gordon 1975; Reubens 1978). Even where there is agreement, however, implementation through this cumbersome and disjointed conglomeration of agencies, lacking any coordinating or directing body, inevitably fragments policy in operation (Weinraub 1980). The consequence is an apparent ineffectiveness, if not aimlessness, in all aspects of border management. As competing agencies pursue their solitary courses, numerous failures and near failures of agency operations occur. The leadership and staff of these organizations are responsive to different constituencies, chosen by different methods, and provided with widely varying amounts and qualities of training and equipment. Each agency has its own means of evaluating the work of its own personnel. Agencies that are not primarily concerned with the border or are not elements of the federal government do not feel part of the border-policy process. Agencies concerned with the distribution of social benefits, such as food stamps, have not considered it their job to apply limitations that may exclude illegal aliens. Local politicians demand reimbursement from the federal government for the socioeconomic costs of illegal aliens admitted by federal laxness in border maintenance. The demoralized INS and its Border Patrol complain that other agencies, or Washington headquarters, are hamstringing their officers for reasons of domestic politics (Carter 1979; Stoddard 1979).

In law enforcement itself division often means divisiveness. State and county police have remained aloof from DEA operations, occasionally interfering with surveillance as a result. The FBI does not work with EPIC. In turn, EPIC is still regarded as a DEA unit and accordingly suffers from the hostility between DEA and Customs, which is still smarting from the loss of much power and prestige by the transfer of drug investigation work to DEA. This interagency bickering has hampered the work of narcotics control, and elsewhere along the border it has led to actual shootouts among federal agents. The divisiveness is at least a partial explanation for the failure to penetrate the weapons-narcotics exchange and for the related suppression of reports on this traffic, even to other federal authorities such as Congress. Much of the cooperation that does occur is the result of informal understandings, mediated by social gatherings and friendships, and consequently vulnerable to change if personalities or ad hoc working agreements change.

Administrative fragmentation in border law enforcement thus has blunted the impact of border policy in one of its major aspects: closure of the border to unauthorized goods and persons. It has wider effects as well, as various agencies pursue different images of the border in their work, depending upon their mission, constituency, and personnel. Local agencies, for example, are thought by federal authorities to be far too permissive or lax in their views of border crossings. This fragmentation is a blueprint for an ineffectual border management, whether of exits or entrances, as various agencies and groups are able to work in the interstices of jumbled lines of power and responsibility, with little or no control or coordination. The personal and policy differences of the leadership in these agencies, which make up the governmental politics of Allison's third model (1971, pp. 144-184), certainly contribute to the confusion, to the extent that some of it reflects personal clashes and power. However, the administrative fragmentation is fundamental; it prevents the formulation of a more coherent border policy and would almost certainly prevent the effective application of such a policy if it should somehow emerge. Thus the organization process of the second model dominates along the border (ibid., pp. 67-100).

A Fragmented Future?

Proposals for administrative reform, which are but a part of a panoply of ideas for changing the nature of the border, range from simply augmenting the existing structure with more money, personnel, or technology to creating new border-management or border-integration agencies, which would be designed to treat the border more clearly as a line of division or a line of contact, respectively. No set of policy preferences coincides with any one administrative strategy. Whatever the intention, the costs of administrative reform can be quite high, evidenced in the most recent effort to realign forces at the border.

Discontents among field offices, primarily in El Paso and San Diego, combined with rising local and national concern about narcotics traffic, violence on the border, and illegal immigration, led to extensive studies by the Office of Drug Abuse Policy under the Office of Management and Budget and to review of and recommendations for change in the administrative arrangements at the border. After nearly two years of work, the papers were taken up for discussion by the cabinet in 1977. In the summer of 1978, reports circulated that agreement had been reached in a rather complex plan, which showed the imprint of much bureaucratic haggling.

The essence of this plan was a departmental swapping of agencies concerned with the border. INS would move from Justice to the Treasury, there to combine with the Customs Patrol; BATF would leave Treasury to join with FBI and DEA work on drugs and firearms traffic. General visa and refugee policy would be lost by the Department of State to Justice, although review of individual applications would remain with the consular service. Not surprisingly, this proposal met with little enthusiasm. Field officers in El Paso pointed out with weary cynicism that the primary problem—lack of overall coordination and direction—would still plague the relocated agencies. Nationally a storm of protest broke as Chicano and other Hispanic activists, congressional committees overseeing affected agencies, State Department officials, INS Commissioner Leonel Castillo, George Meany and the AFL-CIO, and Mexican diplomats expressed vociferous objections to various elements of the proposal. Management specialists noted that years of negotiations to sort out equipment and personnel among the shifting agencies and their subdivisions would be required. Sometime in the late summer of 1978 the reorganization scheme died a quiet, unannounced, but unmistakable death. It was not clear to anyone what, if any, policy would be served by this proposal—if, indeed, there had been any effort to establish such a purpose.

This confusion in present border administration and proposed restructuring may be policy. It is arguable that the apparent divergence between the kind of preferred border as enunciated in Washington and the actuality of its administration at the border is not only acceptable but sought after (Piore 1979, pp. 172-192). Certain preferences are given in response to pressure groups that are active at the center, while others receive priority on the periphery in a never-ending adjustment of the demands of domestic labor and business concerns, foreign-relations issues, and borderlands interests. It then follows that the existing administrative fragmentation is the machinery best suited for the implementation of such policy.

This kind of approach to border issues may be expedient, but it is doubtful that it is prudent or advantageous. As the pressures along and across the border increase, the capacity of such machinery to cope becomes subject to increasing strain. The ability or willingness of the nation as a whole, and the borderlands community in particular, to accept (or even understand) the informal policy in effect, as opposed to the official policy in rhetoric, must correspondingly decline.

Any change in border policy will rest upon the will and the capacity to grapple with the administrative hydra. In turn, bureaucratic reorganization that goes beyond a mere reshuffling of a stacked deck must begin with a better understanding of the implications of various border options and a willingness to discuss and determine these choices candidly and publicly. We may, for example, choose to locate authority for the border in a single agency or official, or create a council of decision makers out of the existing agencies with border responsibilities, which then reports to the president; we may even opt for the present system. The choice, if it is to have any impact, must be predicated upon a particular model of the border. It is equally imperative to understand the effect of the administrative machinery upon the policy; certain choices simply cannot be effectively implemented by the existing machinery. The clearest of such incompatibilities will arise if we move toward an image of the border as both a composite of two nations and a unique cultural and political entity, which cannot be partitioned without untoward damage to the entire community (Whiteford 1979; Stoddard

1979). This model appears to run counter to the entire thrust of international, nation-state politics in the closing decades of the century and to the assumptions of those who work within the structure of the state. It is more probable that the notion of a border as a hard shell will prevail—and exceedingly probable that this view, too, is incompatible with the extant fragmented and permeable border apparatus. The troubles of border policy and administration are likely to continue, regardless of the specifics of new proposals, until circumstances force a radical reform of administrative structure in order to carry out whatever image of the political order has been decided upon as feasible and desirable. With improvements in the organization process and the governmental politics of border policy making, it may then be possible to describe the consequent decisions in more convincing terms as those of a rational actor.

References

Allison, Graham T. 1971. *Essence of Decision: Explaining the Cuban Missile Crisis*. Boston: Little, Brown.

Allison, Graham T., and Szanton, Peter. 1976. *Remaking Foreign Policy: The Organizational Connection*. New York: Basic Books.

Bacchus, William I. 1974. *Foreign Policy and the Bureaucratic Process*. Princeton, N.J.: Princeton University Press.

Bath, C. Richard. 1978. "The El Paso-Ciudad Juárez Region as a Microcosm of the North-South Conflict." Paper presented to the International Studies Association, Washington, D.C., February.

Campbell, John Francis. 1971. *Foreign Affairs Fudge Factory*. New York: Basic Books.

Carter, Marshall. 1979. "Law Enforcement and Federalism." In F.A. Meyer and R. Baker, eds., *Determinants of Law Enforcement Policies*. Lexington, Mass.: Lexington Books, D.C. Heath and Co.

Cornelius, Wayne A. 1977. *Illegal Migration to the United States: Recent Research Findings, Policy Implications, and Research Priorities*. Cambridge, Mass.: Center for International Studies, Massachusetts Institute of Technology.

Corwin, Arthur F., and McCain, Johnny M. 1976. "Wetbackism since 1964." In Arthur F. Corwin, ed., *Immigrants and Immigrants: Perspectives on Mexican Migration in the United States*. Westport, Conn.: Greenwood Press.

Destler, Isaac M. 1972. *Presidents, Bureaucrats and Foreign Policy: The Politics of Organizational Reform*. Princeton, N.J.: Princeton University Press.

Esterline, John H., and Black, Robert. 1975. *Inside Foreign Policy: The*

Department of State Political System and Its Subsystems. Palo Alto, Calif.: Mayfield.

Fernandez, Raul A. 1977. *The United States-Mexico Border: A Politico-Economic Profile*. Notre Dame: University of Notre Dame Press.

Garza, David Trippe, and Cehelsky, Marta, eds. 1979. *Immigation and Public Policy*. Boulder, Colo.: Westview Press.

Gordon, Wendell. 1975. "A Case for a Less Restrictive Border Policy." *Social Science Quarterly* 56 (3 December):485-491.

Halperin, Morton H. 1974. *Bureaucratic Politics and Foreign Policy*. Washington, D.C.: Brookings Institution.

Heclo, Hugh. 1977. *A Government of Strangers: Executive Politics in Washington*. Washington, D.C.: Brookings Institution.

McCormick, James M., and Kilh, Young W. 1979. "Intergovernmental Organizations and Foreign Policy Behavior: Some Empirical Findings." *American Political Science Review* 73 (June):494-504.

Piore, Michael J. 1979. *Birds of Passage: Migrant Labor and Industrial Societies*. Cambridge: Cambridge University Press.

Price, John A. 1971. "International Border Screens and Smuggling." In E.R. Stoddard, ed., *Occasional Papers No. 2*. El Paso: Border-State University Consortium for Latin America.

Reubens, Edwin P. 1978. "Aliens, Jobs, and Immigration Policy." *Public Interest*, no. 51 (Spring):113-134.

Rourke, Francis E. 1973. *Bureaucracy and Foreign Policy*. Baltimore: Johns Hopkins University Press.

Starr, Harvey, and Most, Benjamin A. 1976. "The Substance and Study of Borders in International Relations Research." *International Studies Quarterly* 20 (December):581-620.

Stoddard, Ellwyn R. 1979. *El Paso-Ciudad Juárez Relations and the "Tortilla Curtain": A Study of Local Adaptation to Federal Border Policies*. El Paso: Council on the Arts and Humanities.

Waddle, Paula. 1977. "The Legislative and Judicial Response to the Immigration of Undocumented Workers." *South Texas Journal of Research and the Humanities* 1 (Fall):177-210.

Warwick, Donald P. et al. 1975. *A Theory of Public Bureaucracy: Politics, Personality and Organization in the State Department*. Cambridge, Mass.: Harvard University Press, 1975.

Weinraub, Bernard. 1980. "Immigration Bureaucracy Is Overwhelmed by Its Work." *New York Times*, 15 January, pp. A1, B9.

Whiteford, Linda. 1979. "The Borderland as an Extended Community." In F. Camara and R. Van Kemper, eds., *Migration across Frontiers: Mexico and the United States*. Albany, N.Y.: State University of New York.

Zartman, I. William. 1965. "The Politics of Boundaries in North and West Africa." *Journal of Modern African Studies* 3 (August):155-173.

2 Organizational Variables and Policy Impact: Equal Employment Opportunity

Debra W. Stewart

This chapter explores how administrative-organization practices mediate the impact of equal-employment-opportunity (EEO) policy. The basic assumption is that organizational variables have different effects across policy areas and that the difference occurs in terms of both intensity and direction. Even within a single policy area, equal employment opportunity in this case, such differences might occur across protected groups. A second assumption is that organizational variables, while primary, assume importance in EEO policy impact only under certain other clusters of conditions. Thus the controlling conditions must be articulated in any analysis of organizational variables.

Conditions are ripe for studying factors mediating EEO policy impact. Disillusionment is widespread among advocates of EEO policy. From the vantage point of some researchers sympathetic to affirmative action (AA)-equal employment opportunity (EEO) goals, the policy is simply failing to effect the desired change, and the gains achieved to date are regarded as modest at best (Lepper 1979; Benokraitis and Feagin 1978). (For purposes of this chapter AA and EEO are used interchangeably. Technically EEO refers to the national policy and AA refers to the typical program designed to implement that policy.) Others disagree and buttress their case by pointing to the extensive nationwide network of affirmative-action programs firmly in place in public and private organizations. Nonetheless dissatisfaction with the character of EEO impacts is a dominant theme in the EEO literature.

In this analysis, impact refers to events occurring after a policy enactment and as a consequence of that enactment (Wasby 1970). The critical governmental enactments, constituting the basic legal framework for equal employment opportunity and affirmative action in the United States, are Title VII of the Civil Rights Act of 1964, as amended by the Equal Employment Opportunity Act of 1972, and Executive Order 11246, as amended by E.O. 11375 and E.O. 12086. Policy impact is operationalized in terms of actual increases in opportunity for minority-group members or women evident in an organization. Opportunity is measured by the percentage increase in all positions where concentration or underutilization currently exists.

The basic question asked here is, What factors influence the character of the impact? Three subquestions are addressed. First, what are the conditions under which organizational variables become salient? Second, what specific features of organizations influence EEO policy impact? Third, what does the experience of equal employment opportunity-AA in North Carolina state government suggest about studying the impact of different intervention strategies?

Factors in the Organizational Environment

Van Horn and Van Meter (1977) present a heuristic model depicting eight variable clusters affecting the objectives set forth in a policy decision and propose a set of relationships between and among each. Here six of these variables are treated as conditions under which the organizational variables—labeled by Van Horn and Van Meter as "characteristics of implementing agencies" and "dispositions of implementors"—become salient. This discussion assumes first that in the absence of an EEO enactment at the federal level, organizations will not act independently to promote EEO aggressively—in short, organizations are reactive in this sphere. Second, it assumes that if certain environmental conditions—those most favorable to aggressive EEO implementation—hold, organizational variables become central to interpreting the impact of EEO policy. Once the organizational environment makes some positive response mandatory, the actual character of the impact will depend on an organization's response strategy. Propositions on the relationship among these characteristics in the organization's EEO environment and the salience of the organizational strategies precede an assessment of the current status of each factor.

Resources

The greater the resources available for EEO enforcement and implementation, the more salient the organizational characteristics in shaping impact. The recent restructuring of the EEO effort at the federal level, part of the Carter administration reorganization, has significantly diminished the longstanding problem of duplication of EEO activities by several federal executive branch units. By consolidating all Title VII responsibilities in the Equal Employment Opportunity Commission (EEOC) and all executive order responsibilities in the Department of Labor, new resources became available to each of the principal enforcement institutions.

Standards

The more explicit the guidelines and the administrative directives for implementing policy, the less justification for organizational inaction and the more salient organizational characteristics become in shaping impact. For nearly a decade in the EEO area, ambiguity has reigned over the permissibility of the various employment practices and employers' responsibilities. In mid-1978, EEO standards were strengthened when the four agencies involved in regulating EEO adopted a uniform set of guidelines covering the broad areas of selection in hiring, promotion, and training, so that all employers now are held to the same rule by the enforcement agencies. The net effect of these standards and new EEOC guidelines to be followed by organizations in conducting voluntary affirmative action in order to gain some protection against reverse-discrimination suits has been to reduce the uncertainty in the organization about the implications of conducting EEO-AA actions. Just as organization theory suggests that organizations are more likely to plan when uncertainty in the environment is reduced (Jurkovich 1974), the way for EEO-AA involvement is thereby eased.

Communication

The less ambiguous the communication, the more significant the organizational factors become in shaping EEO impact. The messages and interpretations from the field EEO staff are intimately related to the status of standards that are being communicated and the structure of that communication. Where the communicators are speaking from positions in a variety of agencies, each with relatively meager resources, and where differences of opinion prevail on precisely what the standards require, communication from the vantage point of the organization cannot be clear. With the recent reorganization of the EEO regulatory structure, communications have become less ambiguous, resources for communicating standards have been consolidated, and the standards themselves have become uniform.

Enforcement

The more certain regulators' procedures are to require enforcement, the more significant organizational factors become in shaping response. In the EEO area, enforcement has been achieved previously by a reporting system requiring the submission of data on EEO conditions within an organization. The possibility of court action, in place in its present form since 1972, is in reserve as a sanction against organizations that are not in compliance with the law. The effectiveness of the judicial sanction was strengthened in 1978 when the reorganized EEOC moved forward with new priorities for enforcement action. Since early 1979, the EEOC has been working through its early litigation identification program and systemic discrimination program to identify cases on which to concentrate its energy and resources. In these selected cases, enforcement will be increasingly swift and certain.

Political Environment

The greater are both public and elite support for EEO policy, the more significant an organization's actions become in shaping EEO impact. The political environment obviously varies significantly across organizations and jurisdictions. Where the top leadership of the organization supports EEO and/or where there are significant pressure groups in the community that monitor AA progress, the strategies that organizations pursue become particularly critical.

Economic and Social Conditions

The more the economic environment tolerates the organizational slack to support a generous hiring and promotion program and the more the social environment provides qualified protected group members ready to take advantage of new opportunities, the more significant are conditions within the organization in shaping EEO impact.

Thus there is a dynamic interaction between and among several extraorganizational factors that influences the role they play in policy impact (Van Horn and Van Meter 1977). Those conditions most favorable to effective implementation of EEO policy prevail when resources are being channeled in a nonredundant way, when standards are agreed to by all implementing bodies and thus communicated with a single voice, and when that voice is buttressed by an enforcement mechanism that establishes priorities to achieve the most effective use of its enforcement resources. The effectiveness of the entire enforcement apparatus is magnified if the political and socioeconomic environment is supportive.

The Organization and EEO Policy Impact

Under these extraorganizational conditions, administrative organizations and the people working within them become an important force in shaping policy impact. The question then becomes, What specific features of administrative organization and practice influence the impact? The literature of organization theory and administrative behavior presents two broad but distinct answers.

The first answer comes out of the "people" tradition, which assumes that attitudes, in the form of organization members' feelings, values, and ideas, ultimately account for behavior in organizational life. In the early expressions of this tradition, the human-relations school addressed the importance of relationships of supervisory sensitivity, employee participation, and employee happiness (Roethlisberger and Dickson 1939). Today this theme resonates in a neo-human-relations scholarship suggesting that individual members of organizations have certain personality needs that exercise a direct influence on behavior. The way people understand themselves and the assumptions they hold about the motivations of others are the keys to interpreting behavior in organizational life (Zaleznik and Moment 1964; McGregor 1960; Argyris 1964).

This tradition produces one clear strategy to effect organizational change: focus on individual personality as the source of change. Proponents of this view would admit that it may take a long time between an action directed toward a person from whom change is desired and the point at which that person translates the new insight about self or others into new behavior patterns. Still the belief is that true change will occur only when a new attitude is generated to drive a new behavior.

The second answer to the question about what effects change in organizational life points to the organization itself: its technology, systems and procedures, and controls that structure activity within the organization. The literature supporting this second approach rejects the notion that individual personalities hold the key to organizational change and cites as grounds either that individual personalities are virtually impossible to change without intensive psychotherapy (Chapple and Sayles 1961) or that, even controlling for the difficulty of the subject of the two interventions, structural features are more powerful intervention points (Kanter 1977).

Rooted in a classical theory of organization that sees formal organizational goals (positions) as channeling behavior (Kelly 1969), the contemporary focus on organization itself as the source of change finds expression in work that highlights variables of structure and process as the source of change in the organization. Organizational positions are seen as independent factors that elicit actions rather than merely reflect responses of incumbents. Organizational processes (the work flow and control systems mandated by the tasks of the organization) are viewed as factors informing the range of behavior responses that are possible. This organizational emphasis does not suggest that the individuals are unimportant. Rather it stresses the fact that in the interaction of individuals seeking to meet their own needs and manage their own situations, it is the organizational conditions that incumbents face that set the parameters within which they will act.

EEO Strategies and Models of Organizational Change

The change model implicit in the "people" school of organization theory assumes that an effective change strategy would present an individual with a dilemma of some discomforting information designed to increase that individual's awareness. This new awareness, in turn, would lead to a changed attitude and ultimately produce new behavior. When this theory is applied to affirmative action in an organization, the controlling hypothesis is that attitudes hold the key to understanding limited opportunity in the organization. To produce the effect intended by the EEO policy, one needs to change those attitudes that limit opportunity for minorities and women.

Two sets of attitudes are relevant. First, attitudes of potential victims of discrimination demand attention because an employee's own expectations, confidence level, definition of what is possible, and general self-image may constrain or inhibit that person's own advancement. Second, attitudes of supervisors in organizations, who may stereotype minorities or women in ways directly damaging to EEO, weigh heavily in the opportunity picture presented to minorities and women. The stereotype may emerge in lower expectations for blacks or women, in an uneasy communication between manager and protected group members, or in a manager's perception that blacks or women are distinctly different from the manager (Rosen and Jerdee 1974; Kanter 1977). Whether the attitudinal problem resides in the victim of discrimination or in the perpetrator of discrimination, the logic of intervention is the same: challenge the stereotype, provide information for building a more positive attitude, and hope that pro-EEO action will flow from the change.

The controlling hypothesis in the organizational approach to change, by way of contrast, is that structures within the organization hold the key to why EEO is failing. The effective change strategy to alter the structure and flow of organizational activity would focus on the levers of policies, practices, personnel systems, benefits, communications channels, accountability, and reward systems within the organization. By strategic alterations in these areas, one can transform the objective set of forces that individuals face and thus alter their behavior (Kanter 1977; Gery 1977). This kind of intervention in AA can take one of two forms. First, it can occur at the level of the entire organization through a review of recruitment, work planning and goal setting, performance review, participatory-management structures, benefits, promotions, job enlargement, and career ladders and career pathing, with the thought of enlarging opportunity for everyone, including minorities and women. This intervention can take the form of the development and implementation of an AA program with all organizational interventions designed specifically and exclusively to promote opportunity for women and minorities.

EEO Strategies and Impact:
Directions for Empirical Study

Testing the relative impact of each type of intervention requires categorizing strategies by their intervention rationale and then correlating intervention strategies with changes in the status of minorities and women within organizations. Some exploratory work on EEO-AA in North Carolina state government provides both insights and caveats for future research.

First, the broad types of interventions may be categorized as organizational and attitudinal. Organizational interventions—defined as strategies designed to change the structures, processes, and procedures of the organization rather than the attitudes of its members—can be directed toward general structures, processes, and procedures or can be specifically targeted toward EEO-AA ends. Attitudinal interventions can be directed toward attitudes of managers or of protected group members. Classification of some interventions is straightforward; examples are assertiveness training for women (attitude of protected group member), racism and sexism encounter sessions for managers (attitude of managers), regularized open posting of job opportunities (organizational structure and process), and establishing quantitative objectives for representation of protected-group members in specific jobs (organizational affirmative action). Other interventions are more difficult to classify. For example, an attitudinal intervention directed toward managers, such as a directed feedback of EEO progress information, may actually be carried out within an internal EEO reporting system, a strategy of organizational affirmative action.

The four departments of North Carolina state government where the top leadership was reputed to have a strong EEO-AA commitment were selected for analysis. With the aid of EEO-AA documents and data from interviews with EEO officials in each department, interventions were classified on the basis of a judgment as to the dominant supporting assumptions. These questions were posed in each case: What would you have to believe would change the opportunity structure in an organization to intervene in this way?

Is the intervention directly affecting the organization as a whole in structure or process? Does it directly change attitudes and beliefs of managers? Does it directly change attitudes and beliefs of protected group members? Table 2-1 reflects a set of typical interventions grouped by these categories.

Table 2-1
Types of EEO-AA Interventions in Organizations

Attitudinal Intervention		Organizational Intervention	
Managers	*Protected Group Members*	*Structure, Process, Procedure*	*Affirmative Action Specific*
Sensitize to EEO issues of racism and sexism	Conduct individual career counseling	Post job opportunities	Develop program to upgrade skills, targeting minorities and women
Train in how to provide informal support to protected group members	Disseminate information on successful women and minorities	Maintain comprehensive recruiting system	Review regularly organizational practices to identify disparate effect on minorities or women
Identify managers with attitude problems and counsel individually	Target women or minorities for career-development workshops	Employ routinized method for validation of selection criteria	Establish quantitative objectives for women and minorities in all jobs, levels, functions
Give positive reinforcement to managers successful in EEO	Encourage women and minorities to take educational leave	Maintain an explicit performance-appraisal system oriented to career development	Institute negative reinforcement for managers who fail to meet their goals or whose behavior leads to legal action
Give feedback on EEO progress to managers	Offer assertiveness training	Maintain clear criteria for termination	Require minorities and women to be among those interviewed for any opening
Provide full information to managers about AA program and plan	Establish formal sponsorship systems	Routinize reexamination of job classifications	Develop internal and external reporting systems to monitor EEO progress
			Develop AA-directed recruiting system
			Conduct spot checks in divisions for AA-EEO compliance

On the basis of this admittedly qualitative classification of interventions, each department was located by its dominant intervention philosophy. Operating philosophies vary across the departments and different interventions are associated with different results. In the four departments, the most marked improvement came in the Department of Human Resources, where the operating philosophy called for working through the broad structure of the organization while supplementing that effort with AA-specific interventions that modified organizational structure or practice in some way. Women seem to benefit notably under this intervention strategy. A similar strategy for intervention used in the Department of Transportation yielded a much more modest result overall for minorities and women. In the Department of Natural and Economic Resources, the notable results in minority employment were achieved with only organizational and AA intervention. The Department of Correction, by contrast, operated on a management strategy that adopted AA-specific organizational interventions but tried to alter the attitudes of both supervisors and protected-group members as a strategy. The success the department reports in minority hiring in technical positions and in increasing minorities in professional job classifications may suggest that attitudinal interventions can produce a greater impact in moving minorities into nontraditional jobs than it can in increasing their overall numerical representation.

Two particular caveats are in order for researchers in this area. One obvious difficulty with comparing the impact of interventions across organizations is that the labor-market situation they face varies greatly. In North Carolina, for example, the Human Resources Department labor market for minorities and women is favorable, while the Department of Transportation labor market is unfavorable. The size of an organization also must be considered in assessing the impact of interventions. In a large department, such as the Department of Transportation, a minor percentage gain in a job category may represent a large increase in the absolute number of women or minorities employed. In a large department, a substantially greater organizational effort may be needed to produce a percentage gain equivalent to that same gain in a smaller department.

Conclusion

From a policy perspective, interventions undertaken by organizations merit closer examination as variables mediating the actual impact of EEO-AA policy. The salience of these interventions by organizations will vary depending on the characteristics of the policy environment within which the organization operates. When environmental conditions are such that some kind of organizational action is mandatory, the character of organizational intervention becomes critical. The data from North Carolina state agency experience suggest an approach for categorizing interventions and a word of caution in interpreting effects.

References

Argyris, Chris. 1964. *Intergrating the Individual into the Organization.* New York: Wiley.

Benokraitis, Nijole V., and Feagin, Joe R. 1978. *Affirmative Action and Equal Opportunity: Action, Inaction, Reaction.* Boulder: Westview.

Chapple, Eliot D., and Sayles, Leonard R. 1961. *The Measure of Management: Designing Organizations for Human Effectiveness.* New York: Macmillan.

Gery, Gloria J. 1977. "Equal Opportunity—Planning and Managing the Change Process." *Personnel Journal* 56:184-191, 203.

Jurkovich, Roy. 1974. "A Core Typology of Organizational Environments." *Administrative Science Quarterly* 19:380-394.

Kanter, Rosabeth Moss. 1977. *Men and Women of the Corporation.* New York: Basic Books.

Kelly, Joe. 1969. *Organizational Behavior.* Homewood, Ill.: Irwin.

Lepper, Mary M. 1979. "Affirmative Action: A Policy for Social Equity." Paper presented to the Western Political Science Association.

McGregor, Douglas. 1960. *The Human Side of Enterprise.* New York: McGraw-Hill.

Roethlisberger, Fritz J., and Dickson, William J. 1939. *Management and the Worker.* Cambridge, Mass.: Harvard University Press.

Rosen, B., and Jerdee, T.H. 1974. "The Effects of Applicant's Sex and Difficulty of Job Evaluations of Candidates for Managerial Positions." *Journal of Applied Psychology* 34:234-245.

Van Horn, Carl E., and Van Meter, Donald S. 1977. "The Implementation of Intergovernmental Policy." *Policy Studies Review Annual* 1:97-120.

Wasby, Stephen L. 1970. *The Impact of the United States Supreme Court: Some Perspectives.* Homewood, Ill.: Dorsey.

Zaleznik, A., and Moment, D. 1964. *The Dynamics of Interpersonal Behavior.* New York: Wiley.

3

Human Rights: Administrative Impact of a Symbolic Policy

Harold Molineu

Foreign-policy analysts typically have focused on the formulation stage of the policy process, and thus they have not developed overall approaches and criteria for evaluating implementation. The few existing implementation studies (Bobrow and Stoker 1979) tend to examine a policy's impact abroad; for example, they may look at the effect of a foreign-assistance program on economic development or the consequences of an arms-control policy on the arms race. The criteria for analysis are likely to be of a substantive nature; that is, they measure policy impact in terms of stated goals and emphasize the effect of the policy in terms of the effect of the policy on America's international interests. This approach to assessing foreign policy is rather unsystematic, and it also runs the risk of overlooking more salient indicators of the impact of a policy.

A useful illustration can be derived from a consideration of President Carter's policy on human rights. In broad outline, this policy calls for greater practical observance by foreign governments of such basic human rights as the right to food and shelter and the right to civil and political liberties. A study of the implementation of the policy suggests that it is important not because it fulfills the declared policy goals of improving human rights throughout the world but rather because it deals with the symbolic nature of the human-rights campaign. If one applies subtantive criteria, the international impact has been minimal, but if one instead examines the implementation of the policy in terms of increased bureaucratic visibility serving as a symbolic response to certain domestic demands, the policy may well be considered successful.

An analysis of the way in which the human-rights policy is carried out reveals that substantive, rational criteria may not be sufficient for judging a policy's effectiveness. When a foreign policy is largely symbolic, it is important to understand the extent to which the policy is perceived as being implemented. In the case of human rights, the impact of implementation to date has been felt primarily in the administrative component of the foreign-policy process. The creation of new agencies, bureaucratic reorganization, formalized procedures for reports and reviews, and new personnel designations can demonstrate a commitment to carrying out a policy, especially one that, like human rights, is something of a departure from the past and that has become a cornerstone of an administration's foreign policy.

Thus in assessing the Carter administration's implementation of its human-rights policy, it may be pointless to try to measure its impact on the human condition. Not only would the data be difficult to collect and analyze, but the measurement itself would be somewhat irrelevant to the evaluation. If the implementation speaks to interest groups' concerns, resolves congressional-presidential differences, and legitimizes a new foreign policy, then it may be characterized as successful. And the means by which these concerns and differences have been dealt with have been primarily administrative. By establishing an apparatus and procedures for carrying out a human-rights policy, the administration, and Congress, may well have completed their tasks; the policy has been implemented. What now remains is the maintenance of the new agencies, the preparation of reports, the fighting of jurisdictional battles, and the persistent demonstration that human rights is being taken care of (Edelman 1964, 1977).

Because attempts to induce the Soviet Union to change its human-rights practices by such tactics as restricting trade are unlikely to succeed, it is fruitless to look in that direction for an indication of policy implementation. For example, the probable outcome of U.S. trade restrictions on the Soviet Union would be a reduction in Soviet-American trade, not a change in Soviet domestic behavior. Nevertheless the Carter administration must respond with some gesture or its human-rights policy will be subject to charges of insincerity. Standing firm or engaging in tough debate may be adequate to maintain credibility with domestic interests and the Congress. After all, what ultimately counts to the Carter administration is the American audience, the domestic political payoff, not the Kremlin's actions. Reassurance that the United States is following a humane foreign policy and that it is committed to the traditional values of democracy and human rights can be a major political accomplishment for the Carter administration. The Carter human-rights policy does speak to these symbols of America's proper role in the world, and the activities of the new agencies are testimony that the policy is being implemented.

To argue that a policy ought to be evaluated on the basis of symbols is not to say that substantive implementation does not also occur at times. Some evidence of actual accomplishment can be crucial to establishing the credibility of a policy and in justifying the continued existence and the authority of agencies responsible for the policy. In the area of human rights, sufficient data exist to refute charges that nothing has been achieved, and their periodic presentation can be utilized to reconfirm the impression of progress.

Congress and Human Rights

The initial response to the human-rights problem was the 1973 congressional review of the place of this issue in American foreign policy. At that time, there was a growing reaction, especially in Congress, against what was seen as the cynical, devious, and immoral conduct of foreign policy by the Nixon administration. U.S. support of repressive regimes, prolongation of the Vietnam war, and frustration over Watergate, coupled with publicity about Soviet suppression of dissent and restrictions on emigration of Jews and other minorities, served to focus criticism of the country's foreign policy on humanitarian issues. Moreover human rights was becoming a major international issue both at the Conference on Security and Cooperation in Europe (CSCE), which was underway in Helsinki, and because of the attention given to the Soviet expulsion of major dissidents such as Alexander Solzhenitsyn and Pavel Litvinov.

The 1973 hearings conducted by the International Organizations and Movements Subcommittee, chaired by Congressman Donald Fraser, resulted in twenty-nine specific recommendations on human rights and an amendment to the Foreign Assistance Act, which declares it the policy of the United States "to promote the increased observance of internationally recognized human rights by all countries." Subsequent legislation placed restrictions on military and economic aid to countries engaged in "a consistent pattern of gross violations of human rights." Aid is to be withheld when such action might encourage a government to show more respect for human rights or when the continuation of aid would identify the United States with support for a repressive regime. In addition, the 1974 Foreign Assistance Act (Public Law 93-559) requires the Department of State to "treat human rights factors as a regular part of U.S. foreign policy decision-making" and "to prepare human rights impact statements for all policies which have significant human rights implications."

While one congressional faction was backing restrictions on executive action, another, led by Senator Henry Jackson, was seeking ways to increase the emigration of Jews and other minorities from the Soviet Union. The adoption of the Jackson-Vanik amendment to the 1974 trade agreement with the Soviet Union served as another reminder of Congress's determination to insert itself directly into the foreign-policy process and of its responsiveness to pressures from key constituencies. Secretary of State Henry Kissinger's correct prediction that the agreement would be rejected by the Soviets because of the amendment had no apparent effect on Congress, and although, in fact, the number of Jewish emigrants declined during and immediately after the debate over the amendment, Congress did not change its position (U.S. Department of State 1977). The intensity of congressional commitment to the amendment as symbol, not the actual impact on the emigration of Soviet Jews, thus is one important measure of the effect of this act.

Prior to the presidential campaign of Jimmy Carter, human rights had been introduced as a domestic issue. The success of Congressman Fraser and his allies signaled a change in the congressional climate on foreign policy as an assertive House promised to restore humaneness to the conduct of American policy. This ever-expanding legislation identified Congress, or at least a sizable portion of it, as an audience requiring executive reassurance on human rights and also stood as a symbolic response by Congress itself to the issue of human rights. Legislation is the major device available to Congress for demonstrating its power and for reassuring vocal ethnic groups that action was being taken on human rights. However, although legislation becomes a message to the executive and to the public, it does not guarantee substantive results.

If Congress and key interest groups were domestic audiences demanding action on human rights, the United States, its allies in the North Atlantic Treaty Organnization, and several neutral or nonaligned states constituted an international audience insisting on an American advocacy of human-rights issues at the CSCE. The Nixon administration reluctantly had acquiesced to the inclusion of the humanitarian items on the CSCE agenda and, along with the Soviet Union, originally expected the problem to be handled by a cursory reference to general principles and a reaffirmation of the United Nations Covenants on Human Rights. Washington was chagrined and Moscow frustrated when the Third Basket (the human-rights section) was turned into a detailed and specific set of obligations and declarations of intent. Both superpowers, moreover, expressed fears that other, more important aspects of détente, such as arms control and trade, would be jeopardized by such an approach to human rights.

Nonetheless the increased publicity attracted by Soviet dissidents, the exile of Solzhenitsyn, and the demands for Jewish and minority emigration from the Soviet Union combined to force human rights onto the international agenda. That publicity and the ensuing pressure from various ethnic groups in both North America and Western Europe necessitated some reaction by the Western states. The Helsinki Agreement was the outcome.

Carter's Election Campaign

On the heels of the CSCE and the congressional human-rights innovations came the presidential campaign of Jimmy Carter. The Republican administration was vulnerable to charges of neglect on human rights in light of its actions at CSCE, its opposition to the Jackson amendment, its role in Vietnam, the exposés about the CIA, its support of various repressive regimes from South Korea to Chile, and its neglect of black movements in southern Africa. Without a doubt, human rights was a ready-made campaign issue, a device by which Carter could distinguish his foreign policy from that of Nixon, Ford, and Kissinger. It is important for a presidential candidate to suggest that his policy would be somewhat different from his opponent's, and human rights was a safe issue inasmuch as it did not suggest appeasement or recklessness but did reflect traditional American values.

The consequences of a nation's foreign policy's being out of step with traditional values and self-images cannot be minimized. The American tendency to view the United States as unique, as different from other nations in its commitment to democratic principles and in its unselfishness and fair play, had been threatened by recent events. The public and congressional reaction to Vietnam, for example, was to turn away from the world and to reject that "corrupting" involvement in international politics. Because a president confronted by that sort of attitude cannot expect to have much room for maneuver in world affairs, it is essential to try to synchronize foreign policy with fundamental popular beliefs, and one technique is to appeal to important national symbols. As Charles de Gaulle focused on the grandeur of France's history, President Carter revived democratic values and morality in the tradition of Woodrow Wilson and John F. Kennedy. Despite this déjà vu quality of the human-rights campaign, it was able to serve as a unifying weapon, at least temporarily.

The human-rights issue, consistent as it was with American traditions, served the symbolic function of reassuring the electorate that the country, in spite of Vietnam and Watergate, could still be true to its past and its principles. Given the perceptions in 1976 of popular self-doubt in the United States and the lack of confidence in the government, it was reasonable to expect a widespread positive response to Carter's pledge to put American policy back on the right path.

In addition, the Carter campaign of 1976 also required support from the Democratic party's liberal factions, such as the Fraser subcommittee, which had led the fight in Congress for human rights. The proper stand on human rights, then, was one way to recruit support from a segment of the party of whose loyalty Carter was not assured. Because human rights is such a broad emotional issue and because it can easily have different meanings to different people, it was also a rallying point for conservative Democrats who were making a larger issue out of human rights in the Soviet Union than they were about those in the Third World.

Symbolic Policy and Implementation

A symbolic policy is one that can mobilize support on the basis of rhetoric and gesture, not necessarily through substantive implementation. Thus a policy linked to prevailing perceptions of historical purpose is likely to be well received domestically at a time when those purposes need restating.

However, although presidential and congressional declarations of a commitment to human rights may prove to be sufficient to restore a general belief in American purpose, by themselves such statements cannot sustain confidence in the sincerity of the policy. Consequently in order to evaluate the policy's impact fully, it is essential to move beyond rhetoric so as to measure the concrete demonstration of intent. In the case of the Carter administration, concrete demonstrations are represented more by administrative and procedural innovations than by improvement in human rights abroad.

There is no attempt here to question the motives of those individuals or groups pursuing human rights. Motivation may have been sincere, but whatever the motivation, that the issue emerged and the government began to deal with it is important. The responses of Congress and the White House, for example, may well have been motivated by a belief in the need to improve the human condition, but in the process of response, the issue has become lost in symbol. The driving force of the human-rights movement has been taken up in creating bureaucracies, adopting legislation, and negotiating agreements, which have become substitutes for actual accomplishments. Carrying out the policy abroad is so difficult that it is meaningless to point to that facet of the policy as an indicator of success. Rather success can be measured better by the number of officials and agencies dealing with human rights and the number of legislative acts calling for compliance.

As a result of congressional legislation and President Carter's own initiatives, an elaborate bureaucratic edifice has been constructed to administer human-rights policy. This machinery must operate within a regulatory network specific to the foreign-policy process, although it is not unlike that found in domestic-policy areas. The Department of State has created a new bureau specifically for Human Rights and Humanitarian Affairs, headed by an assistant secretary. The bureau contains the Office of Human Rights, supported by a deputy assistant secretary and a team of newly designated human-rights officers, whose job it is to "implement the administration's intent to make human rights a central element" of U.S. foreign policy. Full-time human-rights officers also have been appointed for each of the department's seven geographical bureaus in order to "assure more effective human rights policy guidance" (U.S. Department of State 1978a). In addition, the Inter-Agency Committee was established to ensure that the various foreign-policy agencies take human-rights factors into consideration in the administration of their activities abroad. Human-rights guidelines were also drawn up for allocation of economic and military assistance, for foreign military sales, and for participation in international financial institutions.

Because the Department of State has not been inclined toward rapid or major reorganization or bureau-creation, its current attention to a human-rights apparatus stands out as rather atypical, suggesting a significant out-side (that is, not traditional State Department) impetus. The political, rather than the bureaucratic, importance of this move is further exemplified by the nature of the initial leadership appointments. Both the assistant secretary, Patricia Derian, and her deputy, Mark Schneider, were selected from outside the foreign-affairs bureaucracy, a strategy that promised to give human rights more visibility than it might have been expected to receive if the appointments had been from the career Foreign Service. Political responsibilities and prominence, therefore, could be said to have taken precedence over reliance on traditional channels for implementation.

Not only must the Department of State conduct its own internal human-rights evaluations, it is required to file periodic impact statements and an-nual country-by-country reviews of human-rights practices with Congress. The stated goal of these procedures is to guarantee that human-rights criteria are considered in the foreign-policy process. By themselves, however, the procedures do not ensure the enhancement of human rights. Even if enforcement action is taken—for example, by the cancellation of aid or military sales—the test of effective implementation is the cancella-tion, not necessarily the inducement of changes in some government's treat-ment of its citizens. The few cases in which the United States has cut off aid, to Uruguay and Ethiopia, for instance, have not produced noticeable im-provement in rights, but they have demonstrated successful implementation of congressional guidelines.

The perception generated by the organizational and procedural innova-tions confirms the U.S. commitment to human rights and helps to establish the credibility of this new policy. The production of human-rights impact statements, for example, may be viewed in itself as a policy outcome. A "good" statement becomes the standard for policy evaluation much in the way environmental-impact statements have come to dominate the implemen-tation of environmental-protection policies, at least according to a scientific community that is becoming frustrated by a bureaucracy's preoccupation with statements rather than with environmental protection (Fairfax 1978).

The other major reflection of the president's human-rights policy is the Commission on Security and Cooperation in Europe. This commission was created by Congress in 1976 as an autonomous legislative agency to follow up the implementation of the Helsinki Agreement. In the nonbinding docu-ment, the United States, the Soviet Union, Canada, and thirty-two Euro-pean states pledged to encourage adherence to certain human-rights prin-ciples, such as the reunification of families, freer travel and migration, improved working conditions for journalists, and expanded movement of information, literature, and students between states. The job of the com-mission and its staff is to monitor compliance with the accord free of the bureaucracy and of congressional committees, although it does report to

Congress. Congress's establishment of such a commission, an independent body with a status similar to that of the General Accounting Office, stands as an innovative and important departure from the normal way of overseeing foreign policy.

In spite of its autonomy, the commission can only monitor and report; it cannot execute. For all of its responsibility and visibility, it possesses no genuine diplomatic or executive authority. Independent of the two main channels for conducting foreign policy, the Department of State and the National Security Council, the commission lacks an operational arm and has no one in the field. But it has become the focal point for examining Soviet and East European violations of the Helsinki Agreement and for looking after the continual meetings and review conferences designed to monitor compliance, and it has also undertaken an assessment of U.S. adherence to the agreement. The importance of the commission's role as the magnet for East-West human-rights issues thus cannot be ignored. Reports to Congress on compliance with the Helsinki Agreement, investigations into human-rights violations, and leadership on delegations to follow-up meetings are handled as much by the commission and its staff as by the normal foreign-policy agencies.

The effect of the commission's influence in the Helsinki process is to allow the traditional foreign-policy bureaucracies to defer East-West human rights to the commission. Because the Department of State was not an enthusiastic advocate of human rights during the negotiations on the Helsinki Agreement and has been a somewhat reluctant participant since, the commission's existence provides a convenient and legitimate means of avoiding responsibility for such an intractable problem as human rights. Indicative of this traditional diplomatic view is the widely, but not universally, held perception that the human-rights drive is an anomaly, a passing fad, and that the department will be grateful when it is able to devote its attention again to the "real" business of foreign policy.[1]

The commission's own assessments confirm the notion that what matters is the process, not the substance of compliance with the Helsinki provisions. According to the commission chairman, the value of the 1977 Belgrade Conference to review the agreement was the full airing of differences and an extensive exchange between East and West on the human-rights issue (Fascell 1978). Although there was no significant evidence that the Soviet Union had moderated in its violations of human rights, and in spite of the fact that the human-rights differences were not even mentioned in the final communiqué, the participants agreed to continue the process by convening a second review conference in Madrid in 1980. The policy thus is being implemented in the form of process perpetuation. That continuation of the debate is taken as evidence of fulfilling the aims of the policy and further underlines the importance of looking at criteria such as symbolic politics when evaluating policy impact.

This argument does not mean that Soviet compliance with the policy embodied in the Helsinki accords may not be measurable or important but rather that the data for such implementation are best evaluated within the context of symbolic politics. In regard to the Helsinki Agreement, for instance, evidence does indicate that some progress has been made, most notably in the areas of family reunification and emigration (U.S. Department of State 1978b). Progress here, however, neither threatens the stability of the regime nor involves basic civil and political liberties such as the right to dissent. Allowing people to travel or emigrate for family reasons does not imply an inherent right to travel because the state remains in full control over exit visas and defines the conditions under which movement is permissible. The principle of government regulation of human activity thereby can be protected while the government complies with some provisions of the Helsinki document. Furthermore, not only can one expect the Soviets to point to their implementation of these selected and safe obligations, but it is also reasonable to assume that the United States too will seize upon these examples as evidence that the Helsinki process is working.

Linking U.S. foreign economic and military assistance to human rights, as required by Congress, is also faced with obstacles to its implementation. The Carter administration has argued that human rights is but one of several considerations in its foreign policy and, as a result, such questions as alliance obligations and security may take precedence. Thus despite charges of human-rights violations, military assistance and/or sales continued to countries such as South Korea and the Philippines and, until 1979, to Iran. One of the strongest stances in favor of human rights by the administration was toward Somoza's Nicaragua, not a country that plays a vital role in American security calculations but one against which sanctions could be imposed with little risk to major U.S. interests. Thus to maintain the credibility of a human-rights drive, safe countries, those with few alternative sources of aid other than America, become targets of convenience, although not necessarily a means of actually enhancing human rights. Tokenism, therefore, confirms the integrity and good intentions of a human-rights policy and undermines the argument that nothing is being accomplished.

For some years, the United States had been seen as unresponsive to the pleas for a stronger effort to end white rule in southern Africa. Tolerance of Portugal's colonial persistence, passage of the Byrd amendment on Rhodesian chrome, and a generally lukewarm opposition to South Africa's racial policies gave the impression that the United States was not concerned about human rights in Africa. The rather sudden shift to support for majority rule in southern Africa by Secretary Kissinger in 1976 was the beginning of a change in American policy, which has culminated in the Carter administration's more assertive effort to identify the United States with black rule.

The crucial component of this new policy is the perception of the United States in Africa. The immediate and peaceful transition from white to black governance would be a bonus; it is not essential. If U.S. influence in Africa is to be credible and effective, American rhetoric and policy must speak to the fundamental grievances and values of black Africans. The U.S. human-rights policy for Africa, with its emphasis on rule by blacks, in spite of its largely symbolic character, is very important in its own right. Symbols in in-ternational politics—one of which is its spokesperson, such as former Am-bassador Andrew Young—define friends and enemies; they cannot be dismissed without threatening the country's position in Africa.

Conclusion

Foreign policies that contain significant elements of ideological rhetoric or that clearly reflect domestic pressures may be assessed more usefully in terms of the impression of movement toward a particular goal than in terms of actual achievement of the objective. Since such policies have meaning for their symbolic responses, it is necessary to consider their implementation ac-cording to the means by which the image of successful execution is pro-jected. In the case of the human-rights policy, the manifestation of im-plementation has been primarily administrative; highly visible agencies and procedures outside the traditional foreign-policy bureaucracies have been created. Thus if one measures the administrative effects, the implementa-tion has had a substantial impact. It may not be necessary to demonstrate international compliance with human-rights standards to assert that the policy has successfully resolved the problem. Inasmuch as the problem was generated largely from within the domestic political arena, it follows that the construction of concrete bureaucratic arrangements may be enough to satisfy the politics of the human-rights question.

The pursuit of human rights in foreign policy contains elements of a long-term risk of creating expectations that cannot be fulfilled. Arousing hopes that U.S. policy is able to promote human rights and democratic pro-cedures sets the scene for widespread disappointment when the interna-tional arena is found to be impervious to American idealism. The post-Versailles disillusionment brought on an American retreat from the world, and although conditions today are quite different, a similar rejection of foreign policy could still occur. Making human rights a benchmark for evaluating U.S. foreign policy requires other governments to change their domestic policies, not their foreign policies, in order for Washington to claim success. The difficulties involved are self-evident.

Nonetheless, there is no doubt that human rights is becoming routinized in American foreign policy. Recently created administrative machinery and procedures will not quickly disappear, and international agreements, such as the Helsinki Agreement, will continue to influence American policy makers. However, once the policy accomplishes its objectives of symbolic reassurance, the intensity of the commitment to further substantive implementation may well diminish as it becomes increasingly difficult to persuade other governments to move beyond marginal compliance. On the other hand, it could be argued that routinization and bureaucratization of the policy are not without impact or substance and that, over time and through diplomacy, a human-rights policy could have impact outside the United States. Institutionalized procedures and goals may, in the short term, be the extent of implementation. In the long term, they could exert a cumulative influence over the behavior of other governments and thus make it possible to evaluate the policy by substantive rather than symbolic criteria.

Note

1. This assessment of the department's mood and its relationship to the Helsinki process is based on my interviews at the Department of State and at the Commission on European Security and Cooperation in March 1977 and June 1978, as well as on my own experience while I was with the U.S. mission to NATO in Brussels at the time the Helsinki Agreement was being negotiated (1973-1975).

References

Bobrow, Davis B., and Stoker, Robert P. 1979. "Evaluation of Foreign Policy." Paper presented to the annual meeting of the International Studies Association, Toronto.

Edelman, Murray. 1964. *The Symbolic Uses of Politics*. Urbana: University of Illinois Press.

_____ . 1977. *Political Language: Words That Succeed and Policies That Fail*. New York: Academic Press.

Fairfax, Sally K. 1978. "A Disaster in the Environmental Movement." *Science* 199:743-747.

Fascell, Dante. 1978. "Did Human Rights Survive Belgrade?" *Foreign Policy* 31:104-118.

U.S. Department of State. 1977. *Third Semi-Annual Report to the Commission on Security and Cooperation in Europe*. Washington, D.C.: Government Printing Office.

_____ . 1978a. *Newsletter* (March):199:24-25.

_____ . 1978b. *Fourth Semi-Annual Report to the Commission on Security and Cooperation in Europe*. Washington, D.C.: Government Printing Office.

4 Antidiscrimination Laws and the Problems of Policy Implementation

M. Margaret Conway

The implementation of a law may result in public policy that is at variance with what the Congress intended when the law was enacted. This can occur in several ways, two of which are examined here. The first is that the regulations produced in the drafting process may result in the alteration of the scope and impact of the policy such that it differs in its effects from what was intended by those who drafted the law. The second is that variations in policy implementation may result from the different problems encountered and different procedures used when a multiplicity of federal agencies are charged with enforcing the regulations. The substantive focus of this analysis is on the Equal Credit Opportunity Act, passed by Congress in 1974, and its amendments, which became effective in March 1977.

Problem of Credit Discrimination

Discrimination in the granting of credit for reasons other than an individual's ability to repay the debt was endemic in the United States until 1976 and aroused the ire of those who were victimized. The attack on credit discrimination was launched from several forums. One was the National Commission on Consumer Credit, which in its 1972 report detailed several types of discrimination against women. These included more-frequent denial of mortgage credit to single women than to single men, denial of credit to a married woman in her own name, unwillingness to count at full value a wife's income when evaluating the creditworthiness of a married couple, and denial of credit to widowed or divorced women. The Congressional Joint Economic Committee spotlighted other types of credit discrimination in its hearings in 1973. Testimony described discrimination against older or retired persons who were denied credit solely on the basis of age, or in the case of retired people of their being unemployed, regardless of their ability to pay any debt incurred. Furthermore discrimination on the basis of race in the granting of credit for both consumer purchases and home mortgages was a serious problem.

A number of bills introduced in the Ninety-third Congress attacked the problem of discrimination in the granting of credit by financial and commercial institutions, but lack of progress in resolving the problem through

35

normal legislative processes led to attaching the initial law, the Equal Credit Opportunity Act (ECOA), as a nongermane Senate rider to a House bill dealing with Truth-in-Lending Act amendments. The rider, which dealt only with discrimination on the basis of sex or marital status, was accepted by the House conferees. The inadequacies of coverage provided by this initial act, as well as other deficiencies in the law, led to enactment in 1976 of amendments that broadened its coverage to prohibit discrimination on the basis of age, race, color, national origin, or because all or part of an applicant's income is derived from public assistance. The amendments also attempted to remedy other perceived defects in the law (Conway 1979).

Regulations to Implement the Equal Credit Opportunity Act

The drafting of regulations to implement the ECOA was assigned to the Federal Reserve Board. The regulation-drafting process stimulated extensive lobbying by both consumer groups and those representing credit-granting financial institutions and businesses. The Federal Reserve Board opened the process to public comment more than it had in previous regulation-drafting activities (Gelb and Palley 1977, 1979). However, inexperience with that stage of the public-policy process may have hampered the effective representation of the interests of those who in the past had been victims of credit discrimination.

The initial draft of Regulation B issued by the Federal Reserve Board in April 1975 had a strong pro-consumer orientation. The criticisms by representatives of credit-granting interests were, however, more effective than the expressions of support by the pro-consumer groups. The revised draft issued in September 1975 modified the regulations heavily in favor of credit-granting institutions and firms, evoking a storm of criticism from representatives of consumer interests, including a number of women's organizations and a delegation of congresswomen who met with members of the Federal Reserve Board. These protests had significant effects on the Federal Reserve Board, and the resulting final draft of regulation B, issued in October 1975, represented a modification of some of the provisions to which representatives of consumer interests had objected (Gelb and Palley 1979). However, in some aspects Regulation B did not reflect the intentions of the drafters of the initial legislation.

A major area in which the regulations as initially written departed from what the Congress originally intended is that of business credit. The 1974 law applied to all classes of business and consumer credit, as the Senate committee report clearly indicates. The report presents the provisions of the bill establishing ECOA, agreed to without objection in the committee, as prohibiting discrimination based on sex or marital status in connection with any consumer credit transaction and prohibiting "discrimination based on sex or marital status in extensions of credit for commercial purposes" (U.S. Senate 1973, p. 18). However, the Federal Reserve Board's Regulation B exempted business credit transactions from requirements of the coverage of the regulations. The Senate committee report on the 1976 amendments to the ECOA recognized that significant differences may exist between consumer and business credit. The amendments therefore authorized post hoc Federal Reserve Board exempting of certain types of business credit transactions from the act's provisions where those provisions are considered unnecessary. The report of the Senate Banking, Housing, and Urban Affairs Committee states:

> The original Equal Credit Opportunity Act, dealing only with discrimination on the grounds of sex or marital status, applied to *all* transactions, not only those involving consumer applicants. The Federal Reserve Board's regulations under that Act have recognized that there are often significant operational differences between consumer and business credit transactions, and this bill permits the Board to exempt classes of business credit transactions where the Act's prohibitions and remedies prove unnecessary.

Persons seeking credit for business or commercial purposes can be affected adversely by the exemptions authorized by the 1976 amendments. The exemptions extend to provisions relating to notifying applicants of the reasons for denial of credit, furnishing to the loan applicant the creditworthiness information used to evaluate eligibility for a loan, and preserving for twenty-five months the records pertaining to a credit application. These exemptions from ECOA's provisions appear to have had a significant impact. For example, incorrect information relating to prior credit history could not be discovered and corrected by a commercial credit applicant (President's Interagency Task Force on Women Business Owners 1978; U.S. Senate 1979).

Implementation Process

Whatever the content of regulations, their impact is a function of how they are implemented, in turn a function of the implementation procedures used by various agencies to which enforcement responsibility is assigned. Administrative enforcement of the ECOA is assigned to eleven different federal agencies for various classes of creditors. Except to the extent that enforcement is specifically assigned to those agencies, compliance with the act's requirements is enforced by the Federal Trade Commission. How can we assess the implementation of ECOA by the various federal agencies?

Factors that should be considered in examining variations in the implementation process for any public policy can include the objective and standards specified in the policy, resources available to the agencies for implementation, intraorganizational communications and enforcement activities, characteristics of implementing agencies, social, economic, and political conditions in the context of which the policy is implemented, and the orientations of the implementors (Van Meter and Van Horn 1975).

The act's policy objectives and standards are specified in both the language of the law and the regulations issued by the Federal Reserve Board to effect the law. Although the resources made available to enable the agency to carry out its assigned responsibilities are crucial to the implementation of any law, none were provided in the legislation. However, the additional tasks assigned to the compliance-enforcement agencies because of consumer-oriented legislation such as the ECOA have resulted in newly created or expanded consumer-affairs offices within the agencies. These changes have been accomplished either by the reassignment of existing personnel or the recruitment of additional personnel.

Intraorganizational communications and enforcement activities require that both the policy's objectives and compliance standards be clear to those who enforce the policy and to the financial institutions to which it applies. Although the Federal Reserve Board's regulations provide a statement of the policy, questions relative to their application have been raised. Communications responding to questions concerning standards of compliance must be accurate and uniform. Individual agencies may respond with an individual interpretation that is not published or with precedent letters that establish an interpretation and provide guidance to other financial institutions that raise the same question. Provision of technical advice and assistance to those who must implement and monitor compliance with the policy is also important, as are effective methods of motivating those who are charged with implementing the policy. The outcome of the implementation process also varies with the characteristics of the agencies assigned the task. These include the size and competence of the staff, implementors' understanding of what the policy requires, their affective reaction (positive, negative, or neutral) toward it, and patterns of organizational control and communication among staff members.

Regulatory-agency personnel tend to develop a strong protectionist orientation toward the clientele that each agency was established to regulate and to focus on safeguarding the soundness and stability of that type of firm or financial institution. Thus the focus of Federal Reserve Board examiners has been on the financial stability of member state banks. Assignment of consumer-protection and civil-rights oversight responsibilities to the examiners created a new role expectation. An evaluation of system-wide compliance performance by member banks with consumer credit-protection laws and regulations commissioned by the Federal Reserve Board reported in May 1978 that the board's bank examiners were more inclined to focus on financial soundness and safe banking practices than on compliance with the ECOA and other consumer-rights legislation by state member banks. The report indicates that examiners were

> unsure of their expertise in the area of civil rights investigation . . . and in some respects there was a mild hostility toward civil rights matters based partly on a perception that devotion of their time and effort to civil rights matters would not materially advance their progress within the system, as it was not an area to which the Board attached great importance, and partly on a lack of confidence in their own knowledge of the rules of construction in the area. [Dennis 1978, p. 9]

Examiners tended to perceive a conflict between monitoring and helping to maintain the financial stability of member banks and the enforcement of civil-rights laws. A major share of responsibility for examiners' difficulties in both attitude and action in enforcing the ECOA and other credit-related civil-rights laws was assigned to inadequate intra-agency training of examiners and failure to develop adequate guidelines and procedures manuals for use by the board's examiners in evaluating the degree to which discrimination in the actual granting of credit was present in a bank's lending practices.

As experience with the enforcement of the ECOA has been acquired, some agencies have decided that relying on consumer complaints and on the examination of records while conducting examinations to ascertain the institutions' financial soundness was inadequate to determine compliance with ECOA. For example, the Federal Reserve Board developed separate procedures for compliance-review audits. These procedures depend, however, on evaluation of records kept by the financial institutions that are being examined. More subtle forms of discrimination, such as discouraging the filing of applications or no written lending policy existing in the bank being examined, result in no written records and hence no evidence within the institution's loan policy and loan application files of any pattern of illegal credit denials.

The implementation problems encountered by the Federal Reserve Board are not unique to it. The Office of the Comptroller of the Currency (OCC), which is responsible for ECOA enforcement among nationally chartered banks, also experienced problems in enforcing the implementation of the ECOA and other consumer-oriented legislation. The perceived deficiencies in its enforcement activities led to a suit by the National Urban League (*National Urban League et al.* v. *Office of the Comptroller of the Currency*). The settlement agreement entered into by the OCC in December 1977 as a condition for dismissal of the suit included a commitment by the

OCC to continue special examiner-training programs and examination procedures. The OCC also committed itself to providing consumer law and enforcement procedures training to all assistant national bank examiners and to require such training as a prerequisite for a commission as a national bank examiner.

An additional task in effective implementation of ECOA is the communication of clear guidelines to credit-granting firms and financial institutions as to what is required in order for them to be in compliance. The regulations themselves provide guidelines, while suits brought under the law provide further guidance as to what is required. However, effective dissemination of information and interpretations by enforcement agencies could provide significant aid and potentially reduce the necessity for judicial proceedings. The mechanisms used for providing this kind of guidance vary significantly among enforcement agencies. They range from individual interpretations sent in response to an inquiry by a particular institution, the predominant method used by the National Credit Union Administration, the Farm Credit Administration, and the Civil Aeronautics Board, and precedent letters relied on by the Comptroller of the Currency, to use of extensive and systematic procedures and guidelines to provide assistance and guidance to regulated institutions, such as those used by the Federal Home Loan Bank Board and those now used by the Federal Reserve Board.

Procedures for handling complaints concerning alleged credit discrimination vary. Some agencies, such as the Federal Trade Commission, centralize the handling of complaints, while others, such as the Federal Reserve Board, decentralize the handling of complaint procedures in the regional reserve banks. Although this second procedure has the virtue of making complaint processing more accessible to the complainant and perhaps stimulating greater attentiveness to local or regional problems, it can also result in a lack of uniformity in the vigor with which complaints are pursued. However, the mere recording of complaints in a centralized docket does not necessarily result in centralized quality control over complaint processing and resolution. Such centralization of control potentially could provide evidence of certain practices that tend to result in credit discrimination and thus suggest the need for revisions in existing laws; an example is the Federal Trade Commission's discovery of the absence of corrective procedures relative to unfair or incorrect credit-reporting practices affecting small businesses. It may also result in identifying a firm or financial institution that is a persistent violator of some section of the ECOA and thus provide the basis for actions to end the unlawful practice.

In its 1978 report to Congress on ECOA enforcement, the OCC noted as a major problem the lack of uniform guidelines for required corrective action when a financial institution was found not to be in compliance. In that year, the agencies regulating the five types of financial institutions drafted uniform guidelines for enforcement of the ECOA in order to overcome the lack-of-uniformity problem. Responding to the problem, the Ninety-fifth Congress enacted the Financial Institutions Regulatory and Interest Rate Control Act. Among the activities carried out as a consequence of that act is the establishment of a task force that is analyzing all nondiscrimination enforcement activity carried out by the five agencies. Based on that research, the task force will issue new recommendations for increasing interagency uniformity in the implementation of the ECOA and other antidiscrimination legislation affecting the regulated financial institutions.

Conclusion

Both the process of regulation-drafting and the implementation processes that have developed in the twelve federal agencies charged with implementing the regulations have had significant impact on the public policy that has evolved as a result of the ECOA. The addition of a consumer-rights enforcement responsibility to the existing and often quite different responsibilities of the regulatory agencies has presented a variety of problems. These have been least troublesome at an agency such as the Federal Trade Commission, which already had an orientation toward the protection of consumer interests. Agencies that in the past have been oriented largely toward monitoring the financial soundness of regulated financial institutions have experienced much greater difficulty in adapting to their new role of enforcing equal-credit-opportunity legislation. The agencies have had to reassign or acquire resources, develop new training programs for personnel, design and put into effect new types of programs designed to monitor the equal-credit-opportunity performance of regulated institutions, and stimulate effective execution of new responsibilities among their own personnel who have often experienced difficulty in accommodating themselves to this new role expectation. It is not surprising that the pace and effectiveness of the implementation process has varied significantly among the twelve federal agencies assigned responsibility for the enforcement of the ECOA.

The impact of antidiscrimination laws such as the ECOA may be delayed as a consequence of the regulations drafted and differences in implementation procedures used by different federal agencies. Depending on the content of regulations, the antidiscrimination laws may result in different policy outcomes from those anticipated by interest groups and members of Congress who supported the passage of these laws. In the case of ECOA, the regulations drafted to implement the law greatly enhance the probability that equal credit opportunity will be extended to consumers but not necessarily to those seeking commercial credit. The treatment received by consumers and the pattern of enforcement experienced by lending institutions also varies by type of financial institution, but efforts now underway may eliminate these discrepancies in the enforcement of the ECOA. The problems of implementation by a multitude of federal agencies are illustrated by an examination of the implementation of the ECOA.

References

Conway, M. Margaret. 1979. "Discrimination and the Law: The Equal Credit Opportunity Act." In M.L. Palley and M.B. Preston, eds., *Race, Sex, and Policy Problems*. Lexington, Mass.: Lexington Books, D.C. Heath and Co.

Dennis, Warren L. 1978. *The Detection and Correction of Credit Discrimination: A Report to the Board of Governors of the Federal Reserve System*. Washington, D.C.: Ottinger and Company.

Equal Credit Opportunity Act. 15 U.S.C. 1691.

Federal Financial Institutions Examination Council. 1980. *Annual Report*. Washington, D.C., 31 March.

Board of Governors. Federal Reserve System. Regulation B. 12 C.F.R. 202.

Gelb, Joyce, and Palley, Marian Lief. 1977. "Women and Interest Group Politics." *American Politics Quarterly* 5 (July):331-352.

_____ . 1979. "Women and Interest Group Politics: A Comparative Analysis of Federal Decision Making." *Journal of Politics* 41 (May):362-392.

National Urban League v.*Office of the Comptroller of the Currency*. 1978. U.S. District Court of the District of Columbia, Stipulation of Dismissal. December.

U.S. Congress. Joint Economic Committee. *Hearings on the Economic Problems of Women before the Joint Economic Committee*. Ninety-third Cong., 1st sess.

U.S. National Commission on Consumer Finance. 1972. *Consumer Credit in the United States*. Washington, D.C.: Government Printing Office.

U.S. President's Interagency Task Force on Women Business Owners. 1978. *The Bottom Line: Unequal Enterprise in America*. Washington, D.C.: Government Printing Office.

U.S. Senate. Banking, Housing, and Urban Affairs Committee. 1973. Senate Report 278, 93d Cong., 1st sess.

_____ . 1976. Senate Report 589. 94th Cong., 2d sess.

Van Meter, Donald S., and Van Horn, Carl E. 1975. "The Policy Implementation Process." *Administration and Society* 6 (February):445-487.

5

Polyarchy and Participation: The Impact of the Voting Rights Act of 1965 in Mississippi

Ronald J. Terchek

Many of the patterns that described the variability of black political participation in the South have changed in the last decade. A high proportion of blacks in a county, once the most potent factor associated with low black political mobilization, has apparently been converted into a resource. Recently fear (Salamon and Van Evera 1973), apathy (Kernell 1973), political organization and competition (Murray and Vedlitz 1975), and socioeconomic factors (Campbell and Feagin 1975) have been used to analyze the variability in black participation in the Deep South. However much these recent studies differed in their explanations about black mobilization, they all showed a significant increase in black participation since the mid-1960s. Indeed black voter registration in the Deep South rose from about 25 percent in 1960, when Donald Matthews and James Prothro (1966) wrote about the new southern politics, to 55 percent in 1965.

Much of the increase in black participation in the South can be traced to the Voting Rights Act of 1965, which was designed to dismantle some of the most restrictive legal impediments to black political participation. With enactment of the Voting Rights Act, the federal government intervened to establish nondiscriminatory standards for participation in federal elections in six southern states. The act suspended literacy tests and other discriminatory voter-registration devices in the area. Moreover, the legislation empowered the U.S. attorney general to designate counties that demonstrated a consistent pattern of voter discrimination and dispatch federal examiners to enroll citizens there as qualified voters. In the examiner counties, the attorney general was also empowered to assign federal personnel to supervise elections (79 Stat. 437).

Within a year after the enactment of the Voting Rights Act, black voter registration significantly increased in the Deep South. In the nonexaminer counties, black registration rose from the pre-Act 1963-1964 figure of 30 percent to 53 percent in 1967 in the Deep South and from 12 percent to 62 percent in the examiner counties (U.S. Commission on Civil Rights 1968, pp. 11-17). A *prima facie* case can be made for attributing increased black registration to the federal intervention variable. However, these figures

43

do not indicate how the act worked in tandem with other conditions, or which factors intensified the impact of the act and which retarded its impact. Possibly some interventionist strategies by the federal government may have only a limited impact because of community characteristics.

To explore the impact of the act on black political participation, one Deep South state, Mississippi, is examined with a model broad enough to consider an array of structural, cultural, and legal characteristics. Robert Dahl's polyarchy model (1971) will be used to consider such conditions as the level and dispersion of socioeconomic resources, the magnitude of inequality, and the historical legacy of discriminatory racial treatment.

Polyarchy

According to Dahl, polyarchy is characterized by high levels of political inclusion (or participation) and competitiveness. In his model, polyarchy is linked with structural, historical, and cultural conditions, which he believes are reasonably discrete. Dahl identifies seven conditions for polyarchical development: historical sequences, the concentration or dispersion of the socioeconomic order, the level of socioeconomic development, equalities and inequalities in the population, subcultural cleavage, the beliefs and tolerance of political activists, and foreign control. These indicators reflect conditions that promote the concentration or dispersion of power, the tolerance or intolerance of elites toward competing groups, and the level of integration or opposition to regime norms.

In his discussion of polyarchy, Dahl examined national regimes, but the model is also applicable to units of government below the nation-state level such as American states or counties, although there are practical problems in applying the polyarchical model to local units of American government. With universal franchise, participation theoretically is inclusive, and there seems to be little variability in the formal restraints to participation today. Moreover, it is not altogether clear that differences in voter turnout can be considered an adequate indicator of polyarchical development in American states or counties. Party competition, issue saliency, political organizations, and a host of other factors undoubtedly account for much of the variability in voter turnout in the United States.

The polyarchical model nevertheless appears applicable to an analysis of black participation in Mississippi. With 7 percent of the blacks and 70 percent of the whites registered in 1964, the state can be considered what Dahl termed a competitive oligarchy with political participation largely restricted to whites. Blacks were excluded from the ballot through the enforcement of a variety of legal and extralegal devices, such as the literacy test and harassment. Extensive black poverty and gross maldistribution of socioeconomic resources further minimized black mobilization. Moreover, in the early 1960s, many local political elites reflected the historical racial norms of the region, and they tolerated a variety of extralegal means and even overt violence to discourage black participation.

Voting Rights Act as an Example of Foreign Intervention

The states of the Union traditionally set their own voter qualifications, bound by broad federal constitutional and judicial restraints, which prohibit exclusion on the basis of sex, race, and other specified considerations. Within those parameters, considerable flexibility is allowed the individual states, and they have implemented a broad array of requirements. At the time of the Voting Rights Act, many of the rules in the South were similar to franchise requirements elsewhere, such as residency rules, but other standards for voter registration and voting were clearly designed to minimize black participation.

In states with literacy tests as a qualification for voting, registrars had discretionary power and used it to prevent blacks from registering. The tests were, in V.O. Key's words, "a fraud and nothing more," seldom applied to whites and generally unfairly administered to blacks (Key 1949, p. 576). The negative impact of franchise requirements was also demonstrated by Matthews and Prothro (1966, pp. 148-156) who controlled for twenty-one socioeconomic community characteristics. They reported that states with stringent voter requirements had lower registration rates than would be predicted on the basis of their community characteristics.

The act, and particularly the examiner and monitoring provisions, can be seen as an example of Dahl's foreign-intervention condition—that is, as control by an outside actor which, in this case, set the rules for political inclusion. Particularly in the examiner counties, local gatekeepers were no longer able to enforce traditional exclusionary standards toward blacks.

Before turning to black participation in Mississippi, it is helpful to consider the level of polyarchical development in the state. Although the 1970 census reported that Mississippi was the poorest state in the Union and had the lowest median education and the highest subcultural cleavage (or proportion of blacks), there was considerable diversity in the state's eighty-two counties, the unit of analysis in this study.[1]

The concentration or dispersal of socioeconomic resources was translated to the level of black occupational vulnerability and tenant farming in 1970. Occupational vulnerability refers to the susceptibility of blacks to white economic pressures. Blacks whose incomes were dependent on local control, such as domestics and farm laborers, were most vulnerable, while professionals and farm owners could be considered much less dependent on local white economic control (Salamon and Van Evera 1973, pp. 1295-1296). On this scale, polyarchical development ranged from 17 percent in the county with the highest polyarchical development to a low of 67 percent in the county with least development.

Family income served as an indicator of socioeconomic development, and here the range spread from $8,548 for the highest-income county to $3,416 for the lowest-income county.

The inequality-equality criterion was measured by the percentage difference in incomes of blacks and whites. For the state at large, black income was 43 percent of white income, but black income stood at 72 percent of white income in the county with the least inequality and was only 27 percent of white income in the county with the greatest inequality.

The percentage of voting-age blacks in a county was used to satisfy the cultural-pluralism criterion, and county black population ranged from 4 to 64 percent.

The historical-development condition was satisfied by the percentage of blacks registered to vote in the 1960-1964 period, with a statewide average of 7 percent and a range of 23 percent to zero.

The examiner program provided a dichotomous measure of foreign control, with examiners present in thirty-one of the state's eighty-two counties.

Not only was there a considerable range in the conditions of polyarchical development, but most polyarchical underdevelopment was concentrated in counties with more than 45 percent voting-age blacks, the areas that traditionally had been most resistant to political participation by blacks. Table 5-1 indicates that on every scale except the intervention indicator, the black-belt counties ranked low on polyarchical development. Therefore counties with a black population over 45 percent will be considered below the polyarchy threshold limit, carrying special disabilities for black political inclusion. Accordingly the data analysis that follows will consider black political mobilization in the state at large, as well as in the counties with a high proportion of blacks, to determine the impact of polyarchical underdevelopment on political inclusion.

Hypotheses and Data

In an effort to determine the factors related to the impact of the act, two hypotheses were tested:

1. As intervention becomes more intense, political inclusion also increases; that is, the examiner program has an important, positive impact on the level of black mobilization.

Table 5-1
Polyarchical Development in Mississippi and Its Counties

Index[a]	State	Subset
Socioeconomic status level (income)		
Below state mean	48%	85%
Average	30	17
Above state mean	22	0
SES dispersion (occupational vulnerability)		
Below state mean	32	71
Average	20	18
Above state mean	48	11
Historical sequences (1964 black registration)		
Below state mean	76	82
Average	7	5
Above state mean	18	13
Inequalities (black income as % of white income)		
Below state mean	48	10
Average	31	55
Above state mean	21	35
Foreign intervention (examiner)		
Yes	41	62
No	59	38
Subcultural pluralism (% black)		
Below state mean	40	0
Average	16	0
Above state mean	44	100

Note: Based on counties with a black voting-age population greater than 45 percent.

[a]"Average" indicates the percentage of counties that fell within ten percentage points of the state mean. "Below state mean" refers to the percentage of counties that fell below the fortieth percentile on the index and had a low polyarchical development. "Above state mean" refers to the percentage of counties that fell above the sixtieth percentile on the index and had a high polyarchical development.

2.   There are limits to the intervention variable. Foreign intervention has less of an impact in jurisdictions with relatively high polyarchical development than in areas with less polyarchical development.

The reasoning behind the first hypothesis is relatively straightforward, but the second hypothesis calls for some elaboration. When developmental conditions are already favorable to polyarchy, changes in any single variable, including the intervention variable, should have only a limited effect. However, when the developmental indicators are low, federal intervention should have a profound effect on the level of political inclusion. In his discussion of socioeconomic development, Dahl used similar reasoning, which also seems to apply to the aggregate scores for polyarchy: "There exists an upper threshold, . . . above which the chances of polyarchy [and of competitive politics] are so high that any further increases in per capita

GNP [and variables associated with such an increase] cannot affect the outcome in any significant way" (1971, pp. 67-68).

Most research on black participation has concentrated on black registration rates, largely because registration figures are readily available and fairly reliable. However, actual voting is a stronger test of participation and represents a more consequential input into the democratic process than registering. In their studies of black mobilization in Mississippi, Salamon and Van Evera (1973, p. 1292), as well as Kernell (1973, p. 1318), used the votes cast for Hubert Humphrey's presidential candidacy in 1968 and Charles Evers's candidacy for governor in 1971 as indicators of black voting. They reported extraordinarily high correlations between the Humphrey vote and that for local black candidates (.92), actual votes for Humphrey and for Evers (.98), and the percentage of the total vote for Humphrey and for Evers (.94). The correlations are impressively high and rest on the widely held view that there was intense racial polarization in the two elections to justify use in this study to measure black voting. The Evers vote in 1971 will be used here as an indicator of black political mobilization in a county.

Two stepwise multiple-regression equations were used in the analysis: one for the state at large and the other for the counties with a large black voting-age population. In each equation, the 1971 vote for Evers served as the dependent variable and the polyarchical indicators served as the independent variable in the equations for the state at large and black-belt counties. In the counties with a high proportion of voting-age blacks, the cultural-pluralism indicator was not used because each of the counties had, by definition, a high level of cultural pluralism.

Results

Political participation by blacks increased substantially throughout Mississippi following the Voting Rights Act of 1965, but the pattern that describes the state at large is not similar to the pattern of participation in the black-belt counties (table 5-2). In the state at large where there was a wide range in polyarchical development, the examiner program played an important but secondary role to contributing to increased black participation, lagging behind the level of socioeconomic concentration as the most important variable. In the black-belt counties, where polyarchical development tended to be uniformly low, political participation was highly sensitive to variations in a variety of different community characteristics, but most especially to the examiner variable. When polyarchical development was high, government intervention was far less dramatic than in environments where political development was relatively low.

Table 5-2
Multiple-Regression Coefficients for Black Voting in Mississippi and in High Black-Population Counties

	Multiple Regression[a]	Beta
Entire state		
Tenant farms	.366	− .477
Examiner	.450	.204
Pluralism	.477	− .166
Income	.486	− .093
Occupational vulnerability	.488	.061
Counties with a black voting age population greater than 45 percent		
Examiner	.535	.578
Occupational vulnerability	.696	.477
Tenant farms	.702	− .040
Income	.718	.235
Inequality	.723	− .211

[a]The multiple-regression coefficients were produced by a step-wise regression procedure whreby each independent variable is successfully introduced into the regression equation according to its respective contribution to the explained variance. The coefficients shown therefore relate to equations that include the independent variable indicated plus all those listed above it.

The federal presence not only reduced the traditional power of local gatekeepers, the intervention variable also helped to alter earlier patterns of perception and behavior for both whites and blacks. Federal agents introduced important disincentives for whites who might have preferred to maintain their political hegemony in black-belt counties, and they simultaneously lowered the risks entailed in and increased the incentives for black participation.

The public-policy implications of this study are suggestive. Certain interventionist strategies by government agencies to increase political inclusion will not have dramatic effects where polyarchical development is already advanced, but in communities with low polyarchical development, strategies designed to enlarge political inclusion will have favorable results. Efforts to increase participation can be expected to be relatively disappointing in areas of relatively low polyarchical development if they are unaccompanied by viable incentives for participation and a strong interventionist presence by the federal government. The examiner program in Mississippi, a highly interventionist strategy for the mid-1960s, brought impressive results because it was applied to areas of greatest need where it was able to bypass local gatekeepers, introduce symbolic and tangible commitments by the federal government, and reduce the risks and costs of participation.

Although other public policies deal with problems different from those with which the Voting Rights Act of 1965 dealt, the results of the act and the examiner program indicate that market mechanisms and benign neglect may be relatively successful in areas where polyarchical development is relatively high, but elsewhere such a strategy is likely to have few positive effects. In view of the fact that many rural areas and central cities, especially of the Northeast and Midwest, rank relatively low on polyarchical indicators, weak efforts there probably will produce few significant results. However, areas with relatively high polyarchical development do not require intense intervention. Since federal resources, including the resource of public support and goodwill for many programs designed to assist those most in need, are limited, it appears prudent to direct federal interventionist efforts in those areas with the greatest potential payoff rather than to dismiss interventionist strategies altogether or insist that every policy uniformly carry a strong interventionist strategy.

Note

1. The social and economic data are from *U.S. Census of Population, General Social and Economic Characteristics: Mississippi* (Washington, D.C.: Government Printing Office, 1971), and *U.S. Census of Agriculture* (Washington, D.C.: Government Printing Office, 1969), vol. 1, p. 33. The percentages of voting-age blacks are taken from U.S. Commission on Civil Rights, *Political Participation* (Washington, D.C.: Government Printing Office, 1968), pp. 244, 247, the same source for identifying examiner counties. The beliefs and tolerance of political elites are not included in this analysis because no reliable data could be obtained for this variable.

References

Campbell, David, and Feagin, Joe R. 1975. "Black Politics in the South: A Descriptive Analysis." *Journal of Politics* 37:129-162.
Dahl, Robert. 1971. *Polyarchy*. New Haven: Yale University Press.
Kernell, Sam. 1973. "Comment: A Re-evaluation of Black Voting in Mississippi." *American Political Science Review* 67:1307-1318.
Key, V.O. 1949. *Southern Politics*. New York: Knopf.
Matthews, Donald, and Prothro, James. 1966. *Negroes and the New Southern Politics*. New York: Harcourt, Brace, and World.
Murray, Richard, and Vedlitz, Arnold. 1975. "Patterns of Political Participation in Five Southern Cities." Paper presented to the Midwest Political Science Association.

Salamon, Lester M., and Van Evera, Stephen. 1973. "Fear, Apathy, and Discrimination: A Test of Three Explanations of Political Participation." *American Political Science Review* 67:1288-1307, 1319-1327.

U.S. Commission on Civil Rights. 1968. *Political Participation*. Washington, D.C.: Government Printing Office.

6

The Bases of Noncompliance with a Policy

Fred S. Coombs

From Congress to school board, policy-making bodies go about their business of shaping public affairs to their own vision of the public interest. Administrators, judges, and other officials may interpret, apply, and enforce in exemplary fashion. Yet in many sectors of the public-policy domain compliance with the resulting policy is at best problematic. Classic examples include widespread noncompliance with Prohibition during the 1920s and abuses of wage and price controls and rationing during World War II. Significant noncompliance exists today across a broad spectrum of public policies, including tax collection, automobile speed limits, marijuana and other drug laws, environmental control, pornography, prostitution, gambling, school desegregation, and even the reporting of campaign contributions by candidates for public office. A sparse literature and almost no empirical research has rendered our understanding of this crucial aspect of the policy process incomplete (Pressman and Wildavsky 1973, pp. 166-168; Anderson 1975, pp. 120-121; Coleman 1975, pp. 19-20).

Consider for a moment the nature of a policy, defined narrowly here as an authoritative communication prescribing a course of action for specified categories of individuals in certain anticipated situations. There will be an authority that formulates and enacts the general prescription, agents who refine the prescription and hold people to it, and certain individuals whose actions the policy is intended to modify. In some cases the target individuals constitute a large segment of the public, such as all operators of motor vehicles. In other cases—much fiscal policy, for example—the target individuals whose behavior the policy is designed to change may be important private or public officials.

For what reasons might a target individual fail to comply with the policy prescriptions? In this chapter I attempt an exhaustive classification of the bases of noncompliance with a policy. The better to understand the utility of such a classification, let us examine the relationship of a policy to its impact. Although I have chosen to emphasize the control aspects of a policy in my definition rather than the objectives sought, most (and perhaps all) policies have goals, either explicit or implicit. In fact, we sometimes use the goal as a shorthand way of referring to a set of policies; examples are the "policy of containment" or "energy-conservation policy." Such packages contain numerous behavioral prescriptions for a variety of people in a variety of

53

situations. Home owners are urged to lower their thermostats, Internal Revenue Service officials are instructed to allow tax credits for home insulation costs, and automobile drivers are forbidden to drive faster than 55 mph. By viewing each of these discrete attempts to change the behavior of target individuals as the focal point of policy, we can then inquire into the implementation of each, by which I mean the extent to which the behavior of target individuals has, in fact, changed in the desired way as a result of the policy. Such a definition may be unorthodox because it refers to results rather than process, but it is useful because it points toward a single criterion of the overall effectiveness of implementation in a single case (Anderson 1975, chap. 4).

Even full compliance, however, may not guarantee that the policy produces consequences of the desired sort. Possibly assumptions about the kind of results that would be produced by compliance are false. Policies that are perfectly implemented may or may not yield the anticipated consequences and will probably lead to an array of unanticipated consequences. Note, however, that for a policy to have the intended impact, there will almost always have been a change in the behavior of target individuals. Implementation may be viewed as a necessary, but not a sufficient, condition of policy impact (Van Horn and Van Meter 1976, p. 46). Thus there are two major questions with respect to whether any policy will achieve its intended impact: Will the behavior of target individuals be changed as prescribed? Will these changes have the desired effects? In this chapter I address only the first of these questions. My perspective is to ask whose behavior policy makers seek to change in fashioning a new policy and then to explore why they might not be successful in changing it.

I will examine five kinds of reasons for noncompliance with a policy. First, failure to comply may be based upon a breakdown in the process by which the prescribed action is communicated to the individual. Cases in which the target individual lacks the requisite resources or ability to carry out the prescription constitute the second basis for noncompliance. The decision as to whether to comply also may be based upon the target individual's assessment of the policy itself. Policy-based noncompliance of this sort may result either from skepticism about whether compliance will gain the ends intended or from disenchantment with the ends themselves. Action-based noncompliance, on the other hand, results when the prescribed action is so onerous to the target individual that it is rejected. The final category is authority-based noncompliance, in which the target individual challenges the authority of the person or institution enacting the policy, or of their agents who are attempting to implement that policy. Kaufman (1973) and Van Horn and Van Meter (1976) suggest roughly parallel schema, although they focus more upon implementing agents in organizations than upon target individuals.

For any one policy there may be differences among individuals as to why they do not comply with the prescription. More important, there are also differences from one policy to the next in the reasons for, as well as the extent of, noncompliance. Better understanding of the bases upon which people fail to comply with a policy should lead to more enlightened implementation and a higher probability of achieving the intended impact. This requires a more thorough examination of the five bases of noncompliance.

Communication-based Noncompliance

That there will be little chance of changing the behavior of any target individual who does not find out about policy changes is readily apparent. The dissemination of policy directives to all of those expected to comply with them is a well-recognized problem in many policy arenas (Wasby 1976). Literate populations and mass communication networks have reduced, but not eliminated, the problem. A more subtle kind of communication problem arises from the fact that virtually every policy prescription is general in form, intended to apply to a subset of individuals and situations. There may be substantial ambiguity, however, as to precisely which individuals are covered, in what situations, and what behavior is expected (Ball 1976, p. 177). One source of such ambiguity is the policy process itself; authorities intentionally leave certain key points ambiguous in an attempt to make the policy more acceptable to political opponents or constituents (Jones 1977, p. 152).

In 1978 the Illinois state legislature considered a minimal competency-testing bill, which would have required the Illinois State Board of Education to develop and implement a testing program designed to promote and assess certain basic competencies for all students. In the face of pressure from teachers' organizations and the state board of education, the sponsor of the bill was persuaded to substitute a much less restrictive bill, which passed handily. The new law said, in effect, that each local district should consider the question and report the results of their deliberations to the state office within two years. Confusion about which law had actually passed, and ambiguity about exactly what was required of whom, persisted for some time among many district school boards and superintendents. Some quickly implemented a testing program under the misimpression that the law required it. Others did nothing, under the misimpression that the intervention by the state superintendent of education got them off the hook entirely.

Bailey and Mosher (1968, p. 99) reported much the same reaction to passage of the Elementary and Secondary Education Act in 1965, where an "initial euphoric reaction" was succeeded by "misunderstanding, confusion and disenchantment":

> Consideration of the legislation had progressed so rapidly that few state
> and local authorities understood the Act's specific provisions or its thrust
> toward certain basic educational changes. Schoolmen were dismayed to
> learn that ESEA was not "general aid." They were confused by the
> technicalities involved in eligibility; they were overwhelmed by the amount
> of paperwork required.

The remedy for communication-based noncompliance would appear to
be policies that are less ambiguous and better communicated with less distortion to target individuals. Ambiguity, however, is one important way in
which some discretion may be preserved for implementing agents, who are
closer to the specific local situation. Case-by-case rulings by judges, administrators, or other agents may be necessary in the early portion of any
policy's life cycle. A certain amount of ambiguity surrounds any policy until
such applications to specific cases have been made over a period of time.

Resource-based Noncompliance

Sometimes target individuals understand what a policy demands of them
but lack the wherewithal to comply. If carrying out the dictates of a policy
demands unavailable funds, talent, time, or energy, the probability of compliance will be low.

The vicissitudes of the legislative process have been known to produce a
mandate for action without providing the resources. Local governments accuse state governments of such perfidy. Private corporations accuse the
federal government of burdensome requirements with respect to converting
plants or disposing of waste, which they claim they are unable to meet. If an
individual, corporation, school system, or governmental unit truly lacks the
funds to comply with a policy decision, implementation will be piecemeal at
best. Nor is resource-based noncompliance limited to financial resources.
Some policies demand skills, expenditure of energy, or mental ability of
target individuals that may not exist.

Remedies for resource-based noncompliance depend upon the resource
in short supply. Inadequate funding may require larger appropriations;
training programs are necessary for policies that demand unusual skills or
changes in long-standing habitual behavior. When it is not feasible to provide the resources or training needed to make compliance with a policy
possible, the policy itself may need to be revised to take account of realities.
For example, there is virtue in keeping tax policy simple enough so that
most taxpayers are capable of understanding and completing their own
returns.

A word of caution is in order before one accepts at face value the claim
that a specific instance on noncompliance is resource-based. It is frequently

to the advantage of target individuals who find a new policy distasteful to claim that they are unable, rather than just unwilling, to comply with its prescription. To the extent that they are believed, the policy may appear unreasonable and ill conceived. The policy researcher should seek independent evidence that the target individual is unable to comply due to a resource problem, and not simply unwilling to comply. Unwillingness would fall within one of the following three categories.

Policy-based Noncompliance

One may refuse to comply with a policy because of misgivings about the policy itself. Noncompliance of this sort is of two basic kinds. In the first variety, the target individual disapproves of the objectives of the policy, or at least accords those objectives low priority in the competition for scarce resources. The parent who refuses to let her child board the school bus in a recently desegregated district because the parent does not value the goal of desegregated schools is an example.

In the second kind of policy-based noncompliance, however, the parent down the street may refuse to let his child board the same bus not because he objects in principle to the goal of desegregated schools but because he does not believe that busing children will achieve desegregation. He reasons that school busing for purposes of racial desegregation will stimulate white flight to the suburbs, thereby leaving inner-city schools even more segregated than before. In effect, he is challenging the assumptions upon which policy makers and their agents based their prescription.

Both of these kinds of objections go to the merits of the policy itself, but the two have quite different implications for remedial action. In the first case of goal-based noncompliance, values are at issue. This brand of noncompliance is difficult to change in the short term, tends to be perceived as a matter of principle, and includes most classic cases of civil disobedience. Such stand-offs are the holy wars of the policy process and occur most often when policy departs sharply from traditional norms and values.

In belief-based noncompliance, on the other hand, it is not values that are in conflict but beliefs about the probable effects of the prescribed behavior. This kind of noncompliance may be changed by appeal to new evidence or expertise that supports the policy maker's assumptions concerning the linkage between prescribed behavior and policy impact. If those assumptions are not supportable, then the noncompliance of target individuals may be well-founded. The early history of Title I of the Elementary and Secondary Education Act of 1965 is strewn with such miscalculations (McLaughlin 1978, p. 162). Even policies based upon sound assumptions may founder, however, if those expected to comply with them cannot be persuaded that the assumptions are correct. Demonstrations of the efficacy of the prescribed approach in other settings may persuade. Testimony from respected experts may persuade. However, just as there are times when collective action cannot wait for consensus upon goals, there are also times when it cannot wait for agreement as to what the probable effects of a certain prescription will be. In those cases, we can expect to see the effort toward reeducation of the target individual replaced by appeals to authority or, that also failing, sanctions. The irony here is that since persuasion through new evidence is in many cases time-consuming and more costly than appeals to authority or the use of power, revision of faulty assumptions held by target populations often is a low priority.

Action-based Noncompliance

In this common type of noncompliance, target individuals may support the goals of the policy and even agree that the action required of them is likely to lead to those goals. However, noncompliance occurs because of the onerous nature of the prescribed action rather than its consequences. Perhaps the clearest case of this kind of noncompliance is a chemical plant that dumps toxic chemicals into nearby waterways in violation of environmental-protection laws (Ball 1976). One must assume that the corporate executives have nothing in principle against the objective of keeping the environment uncontaminated nor do they doubt the effectiveness of the legislation if compliance is obtained. Their underlying reason, rather, is an unwillingness to bear the additional cost of more acceptable forms of waste disposal.

Compliance with some policies—such as taking advantage of a tax break or staying home from work on the Fourth of July—is sheer joy. Compliance with most policies, however, entails costs, economic or psychological, which may dissuade one from scrupulously following the prescription. Few would argue with either the intended or unintended consequences of the 55 mph speed limit: saving gasoline and saving lives (Cook and Scioli 1975, p. 102). Nor is its effectiveness in serious question on either count. Rather, most transgressions are based on impatience with the prescribed action. Conversion to the metric system, rationing of gasoline, and adherence to housing standards embodied in city building codes are isolated examples from a long list of policies vulnerable to action-based noncompliance. Or consider, once again, the two parents who opposed busing of their children. We now see the possibility of still another parent who approves of the goal of school desegregation and believes busing can accomplish it, but still objects strenuously to her child's riding a bus for one or two hours each day to a distant school.

Most policy change requires changed behavior on the part of target individuals. There is frequently a built-in inertia that must be overcome, a phenomenon that has also been noted within organizations in both public and private sectors. New policies create new demands upon the organization and are resisted simply because they require adaptation. We can predict, for example, minimum compliance as a modal response of organizations to affirmative-action policy. Much the same pattern is seen as colleges and universities grudgingly comply with the guidelines of Title IX for women's athletics; resistance is based principally upon attempts to protect budgets and existing programs of male sports.

Upon occasion, action-based noncompliance may involve ethical concerns. More frequently it is a somewhat calculated strategy for saving time, energy, or money. The calculation may include not only the question of what can be gained by circumventing the policy but an assessment of the risks involved. More than any of the other areas, action-based noncompliance is amenable to attempts to provide incentives for compliance. Promises of reward—such as a tax credit—for compliance and threats of punishment—such as a fine or imprisonment—for noncompliance are, I hypothesize, more effective weapons in dealing with action-based noncompliance than they would be against belief-based or goal-based refusals to comply.

Authority-based Noncompliance

Finally, noncompliance may stem from a feeling that the authority that is prescribing the policy, or the authority's agent, is acting illegitimately or will reap undue benefits from the policy. Whenever a refusal to comply has no relationship to the merits of the policy itself but is directed at the regime, legislature, executive agency, or official enacting or interpreting it, we will call the refusal authority-based. The effects of authority can work both ways. It has been widely held that the authority of the U.S. Supreme Court was a major factor in encouraging many southerners to comply with school desegregation policy in the 1960s. By the same token, efforts of the Nixon administration to gain wholehearted compliance with energy-conservation policies enacted during the OPEC oil embargo of 1974 were almost certainly undercut by the administration's weakened legitimacy in the wake of a series of Watergate revelations.

One interesting variant of authority-based noncompliance is the built-in resistance of functionaries at every level of government to policies emanating from a higher level. Mayors and local school superintendents inveigh against the encroachments of state government, question its right to mandate much of anything, and circumvent the prescriptions whenever possible. A similar pattern is frequently observed with respect to the federal-state relationship.

The antidote for authority-based noncompliance is more consensus upon the limits and locus of authority for different kinds of policy (see Ball 1976, p. 178). Power often can substitute for that consensus in the short term, but political systems that experience little difficulty with authority-based noncompliance over the long term have developed elaborate and effective processes for socializing both their citizens and their public officials with respect to a common set of norms.

References

Anderson, James E. 1975. *Public Policy-Making*. New York: Praeger.

Bailey, Stephen K., and Mosher, Edith K. 1968. *ESEA: The Office of Education Administers a Law*. Syracuse, N.Y.: Syracuse University Press.

Ball, Bruce B. 1976. "Water Pollution and Compliance Decision Making." In Charles O. Jones and Robert D. Thomas, eds., *Public Policy Making in a Federal System*. Sage Yearbooks in Politics and Public Policy, vol. 3. Beverly Hills: Sage Publications.

Coleman, James S. 1975. "Problems of Conceptualization and Measurement in Studying Policy Impacts." In Kenneth M. Dolbeare, ed., *Public Policy Evaluation*. Sage Yearbooks in Politics and Public Policy, vol. 2. Beverly Hills: Sage Publications.

Cook, Thomas J., and Scioli, Frank P., Jr., 1975. "Impact Analysis in Public Policy Research." In Kenneth Dolbeare, ed., *Public Policy Evaluation*. Sage Yearbooks in Politics and Public Policy, vol. 2. Beverly Hills: Sage Publications.

Jones, Charles O. 1977. *An Introduction to the Study of Public Policy*. 2d ed. North Scituate, Mass.: Duxbury Press.

Kaufman, Herbert. 1973. *Administrative Feedback*. Washington, D.C.: Brookings Institution.

McLaughlin, Milbrey Wallin. 1978. "Implementation of ESEA Title I: A Problem of Compliance." In Dale Mann, ed., *Making Change Happen?* New York: Teachers College Press.

Mann, Dale, ed. 1978. *Making Change Happen?* New York: Teachers College Press.

Milward, H. Brinton, and Swanson, Cheryl. 1978. "The Impact of Affirmative Action on Organizational Behavior." *Policy Studies Journal* 7 (Winter):201-207.

Pressman, Jeffrey L., and Wildavsky, Aaron B. 1973. *Implementation: How Great Expectations in Washington Are Dashed in Oakland . . .* Berkeley: University of California Press.

Van Horn, Carl E., and Van Meter, Donald S. 1976. "The Implementation of Intergovernmental Policy." In Charles O. Jones and Robert D. Thomas, eds., *Public Policy Making in a Federal System*. Sage Yearbooks in Politics and Public Policy, vol. 3. Beverly Hills: Sage Publications.

Wasby, Stephen L. 1976. *Small Town Police and the Supreme Court: Hearing the Word*. Lexington, Mass.: Lexington Books, D.C. Heath and Co.

Part II
Unintended Impacts
of Policies

The chapters in this part deal with the unintended consequences of policies. One deals with urban development; the other three focus on federalism. In her examination of three California cities during the 1970s, Phyllis Strong Green, instead of assessing only the effect of the adopted policy, looks beyond it to inputs that were not anticipated by those who set the policy. She then examines both unanticipated impacts and indirect consequences of growth-management policy, paying particular attention to intergovernmental impacts. Federal-local intergovernmental relations are the focus of the chapters by William Hudson, E. Terrence Jones, and Edmund Beard and Peter DiToro. Hudson, using El Paso, Texas, as a case study, shows that the revenue-sharing and block-grant components of the New Federalism made the city more, not less, dependent on the national government, despite the goal of New Federalism to increase political decentralization. Jones examines block grants for community development and CETA in St. Louis City and St. Louis County and shows how differences in the local polities that were expending these grants affect policy implementation and impact. Like Hudson, he suggests the constraining effects of national policy on local autonomy. Edmund Beard's and Peter DiToro's study shows how great expectations in Washington are dashed in Boston. Section 8 of the Housing and Community Development Act of 1974, which was designed to discourage segregation, appears to be promoting it, due to the use of Section 8 funds to further the process of gentrification in a mixed community. The results of the interplay of local interest groups were unanticipated, and thus the law's impact was not as intended.

7 Confounding Influences, Unintended Impacts, and Growth-Management Policies

Phyllis Strong Green

A basic dilemma for policy makers is how to control policy impacts once the implementation process has begun. In some areas, the policy itself seems to take on a life of its own, apart from the control that public officials exercise over it. Like a runaway car, it careens here and there until it lands on steady ground, sometimes running through barriers and circumventing other obstacles along the way.

This study examines the unanticipated inputs, unintended consequences, and indirect effects of growth-management policies that were adopted and implemented in three rapidly growing representative California cities, Petaluma, San Diego, and Modesto, during the period 1970-1979. The study addresses the question posed by Austin Ranney (1968, p. 7) of how closely the implementation of intent (that is, actions taken to pursue policy objectives) approximates the declaration of intent.

To answer this question, it is necessary to examine why implementation does not take place as it is intended to, or what factors confound the implementation process, and what unforeseen consequences occur once the implementation process is in effect. Blalock (1972, pp. 184-188) uses the term *confounding influences* to denote alternative explanations for observed policy outcomes. For purposes of this study, confounding influences are defined as unanticipated inputs into a policy that frustrate implementation, while unintended impacts are synonymous with the unanticipated outputs that often frustrate the intent of the policy.

It can be hypothesized that many of the problems of policy implementation occur within the policy-making jurisdictions and are internal problems of organization, priority setting, and coordination. Once policy actions are taken to implement the policy, problems external to the policy-making environment intrude, producing inputs that are antithetical to the intentions of policy makers.

Methods of the Study

Data used in this analysis were obtained from three types of sources: personal in-depth interviews with over sixty political actors, including govern-

65

ment officials, outside consultants, and representatives of development, environmental, and citizen groups and advisory boards; public documents and newspapers; and observation of meetings on growth management in the city of San Diego for a period of more than two years.

Policy Intent

Growth-managment policies were designed to deal with problems relating to rapid subdivision development in fringe areas of cities that citizens and public officials perceived as overtaxing fiscal and environmental resources and impinging upon the quality of life. In 1972 Petaluma, a small suburban community near San Francisco in northern California, had chosen a five-hundred-unit annual building-quota policy. Modesto, the county seat of predominantly agricultural Stanislaus County in central California, had a population of seventy-five thousand when it adopted a sewer trunk extension policy in 1974. San Diego, the ninth largest city in the nation, is the southernmost city in the state. From 1970 to 1974 it incrementally adopted a phased-growth policy, which tied development to the availability of capital facilities. In 1979 the series of policies was synthesized into a comprehensive growth-management policy.

From the outset, the three cities recognized the need for policy coordination with the county and/or school districts in order to mitigate spillover effects. The policies of Petaluma and San Diego included school districts early in the policy-making process, while school representation came later in Modesto. Stanislaus County cooperated with the city of Modesto at the policy-formulation stage, using its general plan, zoning, and annexation powers as the basis for a complementary growth policy. The policy required that annexation of proposed subdivisions be limited to incorporated cities or sewer districts in unincorporated towns. It was not until 1979 that Sonoma County and San Diego County adopted their own growth policies with similar objectives to those of Petaluma and the city of San Diego.

Nature of Anticipated Effects

Public officials in the three cities anticipated positive fiscal and environmental impacts from policy actions, while readily admitting the uncertainty of potential economic ones. They anticipated a number of short-term effects, such as in-filling of vacant land to divert new housing construction to older areas of the city where capital facilities were already established; acquisition of open-space parks and preservation of prime agricultural land in outlying areas of the city and county; and alleviation of school over-crowding and road congestion.

Policymakers argued that any negative economic impacts that would be generated by restrictions on housing supply, such as a rise in housing and land prices, and construction industry unemployment would be carefully monitored and held to a minimum. Planners viewed growth management as an opportunity for the innovative use of traditional and recently devised planning, regulatory, fiscal-management techniques, and private-sector incentives in the actual implementation of general plans.

The importance to public officials of gathering information on fiscal, environmental, and economic impacts can be discerned by the fact that all three cities hired professional consulting firms to conduct formal studies in one or more of these areas. In the San Diego metropolitan area, economic studies were also commissioned by the construction industry federation and a regional planning organization, and in-house studies were conducted at the city and county government level.

Strategy and Actions

Policy makers in the three cities sought to use private incentives to promote public purposes, such as optimal use of existing capital facilities and construction of needed multifamily and moderate-income housing. In order to make land costs competitive, city councils in Modesto and San Diego tried to narrow the gap between costly land in the central city and less-expensive land in the outlying areas. They modified zoning ordinances and building codes to facilitate higher-density housing in the older, established areas. San Diego officials imposed user fees, partly as a disincentive against developers' building in outlying areas, and waived development fees in the central city. They also attempted to reduce the cost of locating in the older areas by reducing permit-processing time, eliminating the appeals process for environmental-impact reports, simplifying review procedures, and reducing parking-space requirements and lot size. Such changes have long been recommended by housing-policy analysts as incentives that would facilitate low- and moderate-income housing (Davidoff and Brooks 1976; Danielson 1976).

The Residential Development Board in Petaluma faithfully adhered to the annual city-council policy resolution that allotted the same number of multifamily and single-family housing in the eastern and western sections of the city. The strategy was intended to divert builder preferences from single-family houses to multifamily dwellings. Petaluma officials also offered incentives to developers to build below-market units for moderate-income buyers. Yet despite these selective incentives, Petaluma and San Diego found the policy implementation process being obstructed by a number of confounding inputs, while Modesto officials were able to control these inputs.

Confounding Policy Inputs

City-council members and planners in Petaluma and San Diego discovered during the implementation process that a number of unforeseen events worked against their policy objectives. Findings of this study suggest that these unintended impacts can be traced to the ways that policy makers used their resources. Policy inputs confound implementation under at least three conditions: when policy makers delegate authority to other jurisdictions and are unaware of how such authority is being used, when government officials inflexibly apply rules and regulations without regard to economic and political conditions, and when poor communication exists between public officials and affected interests.

The first condition was exemplified in the city of San Diego when a major policy objective, in-filling in the central city, was blocked by school officials. The city council had delegated to the San Diego Unified School District virtual veto power over new housing development by granting authority to issue a letter of school availability. Used in conjunction with public hearings, the letter worked to scuttle or delay housing construction in the older, established areas of the city. Qualifying criteria were so inflexibly applied that few developers could comply. This policy action not only obstructed the in-filling objective but also produced a temporary housing shortage throughout the city. Once this outcome was recognized, however, city officials reclaimed control over development.

Petaluma's Residential Development Evaluation Board, like the San Diego school board, applied rules and regulations inflexibly. The board rigidly adhered to the annual allotments set each year by city-council resolution and to the rule that no single developer could apply to build more than one hundred units. There was no consideration of the economics of the housing industry or numbers of applications by category. More specifically, the board failed to take advantage of the high number of applications for multifamily housing in one year, a pattern that did not repeat itself in subsequent years. Thus after three years of actual policy implementation, Petaluma faced a backlog of 1,180 unbuilt houses and, therefore, unattained quotas. Moreover, by December 1979 not a single unit of housing for the low- and moderate-income market had been built under the growth-management policy, which had allocated 8 to 12 percent of housing in this category. (Some of the allocated moderate-income housing may be provided by 142 below median-market-price units that were in various stages of construction in early 1980.) City planners argued that economic conditions (citing, for example, "builder financing problems") and not public policy were responsible for these outcomes. An alternative explanation, however, is that the city council's limitation on housing units per developer eliminated large-scale developers for whom it would have been most financially feasible to absorb the cost of below-market units.

A third confounding input was citizen participation in public hearings on rezoning to facilitate higher-density housing in Modesto and San Diego. Community-planning groups in San Diego were particularly vocal in opposing rezoning and other changes in housing requirements, actions that they believed benefited developers and not the city. This opposition has been attributed to Proposition 13 cutbacks and resignations, which had reduced the number of community planners to a point where they could not adequately inform the city's thirty community-planning groups about city-wide objectives. This observation is in keeping with Wasby's (1976) finding that effective communication between decision makers and affected interests is a key process in winning compliance with governmental directives.

Intended Impacts

The consensus of city and county officials was that in-filling was the most import achievement of growth management, an outcome that produced optimal use of existing capital facilities, as well as needed multifamily housing. In all three cities, growth management generated new housing in older, established areas where new housing had not been built for years. In San Diego, the only verifiable result of two professional studies of the economic impacts of growth management was an increase in multifamily housing at the expense of single-family dwellings.

Even so there is evidence that the in-filling objective was not caused by growth management, although it was accelerated under it. City planners concede that in-filling would have occurred even without growth management, although at a slower rate, due to rising gasoline prices that serve as a disincentive to commute and the inflation-induced rise in land costs in outlying areas to levels roughly at parity with city lots. It is fair to conclude, however, that the implementation of growth-management policies sets the direction for the construction of new housing in the central city.

A temporary slowdown in housing construction helped to alleviate school overcrowding and road congestion in Petaluma and sections of San Diego. However, decisions of the California Transportation Agency were intervening variables in city decisions to upgrade access roads that would link with projected state highways. Moreover, state court decisions on school integration and financing appeared to have a greater impact on the housing and distribution of school children than did growth-management policies.

A cause-and-effect relationship could not be established between growth management and environmental impacts, such as the acquisition of open-space parks and the effect of state tax incentives on the amount of acreage placed in agricultural preserves in Stanislaus County. Exogenous variables that obscured relationships in economic-impact analyses were even more important in environmental-impact analyses because of the longer time frame needed to detect change. This fact validates Wilson's (1973, p. 133) conclusion that studies that adopt a short time frame minimize the chance for desired effects to appear and maximize the need to search for other variables that might explain the observed facts.

Unintended Consequences

Developers in Modesto and San Diego contended that growth management would result in an inadequate housing supply and high unemployment in the construction industry. They correctly argued that the inventory of land in the central city was not adequate to meet the demand for new housing. While construction-industry unemployment proved to be only temporary in nature, the housing supply was unable to keep up with demand. Nevertheless, there is insufficient evidence to link growth management to a long-term housing shortage. National problems of inflation, high financing costs, and the volatile nature of housing construction cycles obscure the cause-and-effect relationship between government regulations that raise housing costs and a shortage in housing supply. Consequently the difficulty identified by Dolbeare (1974, p. 115) of sorting out which policy components bring about which consequences is particularly applicable in this case.

An unintended impact of Proposition 13 may be to raise the price of housing by forcing new developments in outlying areas to pay their own way. Under growth management, user fees increasingly are being used in conjunction with special tax-assessment districts to pay for capital improvements as well as for operating expenses. Since these expenses are generally passed on to consumers, many home buyers and renters are likely to be priced out of the new housing market, making much of this housing accessible only to the affluent.

According to San Diego city planners, an unintended but not undesired impact of the in-filling strategy there was to make small developers competitive with large developers, a fact that may have helped to implement the in-filling objective. Planners in Modesto and San Diego also suggest that the in-filling process is making some modest changes by race and income in sections of those two cities. However, given escalating home-mortgage interest rates at the end of 1979, it did not appear that private-sector incentives would be sufficient to generate affordable housing for moderate-income buyers in the central city.

Indirect Impacts

A shift of fiscal problems to other local jurisdictions is an indirect effect of policies that restrict housing supply in a high-demand area. Housing demand in metropolitan areas is not amenable to short-term manipulation. If there is a strong demand in one geographical location and the housing supply is limited by natural or artificial forces (such as government actions), then builders fill the demand by building in contiguous areas. The domino theory as applied to land economics states that locational decisions in independent governmental jurisdictions will invariably generate spillover effects on other jurisdictions.

Intergovernmental Impacts

Since impacts may be intergovernmental, several direct and indirect policy impacts on counties, municipalities, and school districts can be traced to growth-management policies in the cities of Petaluma and San Diego. Under the coordinated policy of Modesto and Stanislaus County, schools were largely unaffected, but two patterns emerged during policy implementation in Sonoma and San Diego counties.

The first pattern characterizes a number of cities that have adopted growth-management policies. For example, rigid growth restrictions in Petaluma and San Diego forced developers into Rohnert Park, a city adjacent to Petaluma in the San Francisco metropolitan area, and into Poway, an unincorporated community bordering a fast-growing area within the city of San Diego. An increase in the demand for housing occurred within these communities, followed by overcrowded schools and road congestion. Parent organizations protested school overcrowding, and the school board adopted emergency measures, among them double sessions. Referenda to approve bonds for new school construction failed to win voter approval. Subsequently joint action was taken by the Rohnert Park city council and school board, which imposed a temporary moratorium on subdivision development, followed by the payment of school fees as a condition for issuing building permits. The San Diego County Board of Supervisors and the Poway Unified School District took similar action. Subsequently the city of Rohnert Park and the county of San Diego adopted their own growth-management policies.

The second pattern emerges when the actions of one governmental unit intentionally or unintentionally generate changes in the power structure of another governmental unit. There appears to be a strong association, in this pattern, between growth-management policies, as they are translated into the politics of land use, and subsequent political upheavals in neighboring jurisdictions. In Sonoma and San Diego counties, interest-group activity was a strong contributing factor in political change. For example, subdivision developers and builders, as targets of growth-management policies in Petaluma and San Diego, found their influence over city governments to be restricted. Consequently the Homebuilders' Association in Sonoma County turned its attention to the election of growth-oriented members of the county board of supervisors. In San Diego County, environmental coalitions formed in the city were reactivated at the county level, and the mayor of San Diego publicly endorsed a county supervisorial candidate who favored growth management. The issue was kept before the public through metropolitan-area newspaper and television coverage prior to elections in contiguous jurisdictions in which growth was an issue, an example of placing policy issues on the public agenda by widening the scope of controversy (Schattschneider 1960, pp. 16-18).

While the Petaluma and Modesto city councils did not try to influence county politics, the San Diego City Council majority aggressively sought to expand its territorial influence over neighboring jurisdictions through its control of the metropolitan sewerage system. This form of urban imperialism was pursued with the explicit intent of engendering regional cooperation by spurring the adoption of compatible growth-management policies in contiguous jurisdictions. The strategy accelerated county efforts to produce a growth-management policy.

When the county policy was adopted, city and county officials made little attempt to coordinate policy objectives, identify areas of potential conflict, and negotiate priorities. Under these conditions, there was no assurance that policy actions would be compatible or spillover effects mitigated. The issue came to a head in 1979 when the housing shortage in San Diego led to the city council's approval of a 14,000-unit planned community, North City West. The proposed development would be adjacent to a small north-shore city and to unincorporated communities in the county of San Diego. Officials of the county and affected communities claimed that the development violated the city's stated policy objectives, even though the developers were required to provide all capital facilities. They argued that the first increments of the huge development would generate school overcrowding, road congestion, air pollution, and damage to agricultural crops, which would, in turn, promote the premature development of farmland (Zucker 1979).

The county and north-shore city threatened court action and appealed to the Air Quality Board to review the potential impact of the planned community on the air quality of the region. The county's response to city actions reveals that local governments that are large enough and bold enough to exert their influence extraterritorially to protect the integrity of their policies run the risk of counterattacks from other powerful jurisdictions intent on protecting the integrity of their own policies. Consequently unilateral policy decisions may turn out to be counterproductive, while joint consultation in priority setting is more likely to produce mutually acceptable results.

Conclusion

Although public officials may have limited control over inputs and outputs, the findings of this study suggest that they can minimize confounding influences and unintended impacts by giving greater attention to four factors:

1. A clear division of responsibilities to maximize accountability and minimize the proclivity to share the blame with other jurisdictions, which can prove to be counterproductive.
2. Effective communication among public officials in counties, cities, and school districts in which areas of high and low priority are identified.
3. Agreement on priorities through negotiation and coordination of proposed policy actions that could impose negative spillover effects on other jurisdictions.
4. Flexibility in rule application with greater knowledge of and concern for housing economics and market conditions.

Problems that emerged in the cities of Petaluma and San Diego with county and school-district officials were precluded in Modesto and Stanislaus County because the city and county were able to work out complementary growth policies early in the policy-making process. The sewer-extension policy allowed the city to control housing distribution without causing a shortage in the housing supply, while county restrictions on annexations minimized spillover effects on contiguous jurisdictions. In contrast, controls on housing supply in Petaluma produced a shortfall in the allotted housing supply in terms of location, type, and price level. Delegation of authority by the city of San Diego to the San Diego Unified School District to determine availability of capital facilities almost scuttled the city's in-filling objective. Opposition to in-filling by community-planning groups further demonstrated poor communication between city officials and affected interests. These facts support the thesis of Van Meter and Van Horn (1975, p. 466) that "the prospects of effective implementation will be enhanced by the clarity with which standards and objectives are stated and by the accuracy and consistency with which they are communicated."

While the citizen board in Petaluma merely conformed to city-council policy, the school board in San Diego interpreted the city's policy inflexibly to suit its own objectives, which were not in accordance with the city's priorities. School-board actions led to a shortage of housing in the desired locations. Bottled-up demand in Petaluma and San Diego, in turn, imposed negative externalities on neighboring jurisdictions. Friction between the county and city of San Diego grew out of these spillover effects and a lack of negotiated priorities and coordinated policy objectives.

This study does not suggest that growth-management policies in San Diego and Petaluma were less successful than those of Modesto and Stanislaus County, nor does it imply that Modesto's approach can be generalized to other cities. Too many exogenous variables preclude such an application. The environments in which public officials make policy decisions impose constraints on some decisions and provide opportunities for others. Moreover, given the information that is generated in a case-study approach, it is difficult to trace cause-and-effect relationships with any degree of accuracy. Policy makers can, however, use this information to attempt to make policy implementation more closely approximate intended policy objectives.

References

Blalock, Hubert M., Jr. 1972. *Causal Inferences in Nonexperimental Research*. New York: Norton Library Edition.

Danielson, Michael N. 1976. *The Politics of Exclusion*. New York: Columbia University Press.

Davidoff, Paul, and Brooks, Mary E. 1976. "Zoning Out the Poor." In Phillip C. Dolce, ed., *Suburbia*. Garden City, N.Y.: Doubleday, Anchor Books.

Dolbeare, Kenneth M. 1974. "The Impacts of Public Policy." In Cornelius P. Cotter, ed., *The Political Science Annual, 1974*. Indianapolis: Bobbs-Merrill.

Ranney, Austin, ed. 1968. *Political Science and Public Policy*. Chicago: Markham.

Schattschneider, E.E. 1960. *The Semisovereign People*. New York: Holt, Rinehart and Winston.

Van Meter, Donald S., and Van Horn, Carl E. 1975. "The Policy Implementation Process." *Administration and Society* 6 (February):445-487.

Wasby, Stephen L. 1976. *Small Town Police and the Supreme Court*. Lexington, Mass.: Lexington Books, D.C. Heath and Co.

Wilson, James Q. 1973. "On Pettigrew and Armor." *Public Interest* 30 (Winter):132-134.

Zucker, Paul C. 1979. *Review of City of San Diego Growth Management Plan*. San Diego: County of San Diego Integrated Planning Office, 16 February.

8 The New Federalism Paradox

William E. Hudson

When President Richard Nixon proposed his New Federalism reforms in his first term, he explained his aim as the reversal of "the trend toward more centralization of government in Washington" (Nathan 1975, p. 102). In order to accomplish this purpose, the New Federalism was intended to increase the discretion of state and local decision makers over the expenditure of federal funds by shifting from categorical grants-in-aid to revenue-sharing and block grants. Decentralization was the central objective of the New Federalism (Thompson 1973), but final support for the reforms came from a diverse coalition advocating multiple objectives, from improved local coordination to improved fiscal balance between governments (Caputo and Cole 1974, pp. 19-22). For the most part, political conservatives emphasized decentralization, although liberals also saw revenue sharing as "revitalizing state and local governments" (Heller 1968, pp. 17-20). Despite these diverse objectives, all policy makers seemed to think that insofar as the New Federalism affected intergovernmental political relationships, it would promote more state and local autonomy in dealing with local problems.

At the local government level, New Federalism grants were supposed to promote more local autonomy because they would be distributed on the basis of legislative formula, and their guidelines would give city officials greater flexibility in using the money. Some studies of New Federalism programs seemed to be based on the assumption that increased discretion of local administrators in spending New Federalism money by definition accomplishes decentralization (Nathan and Adams 1977, pp. 164-165). During the 1960s cities had to compete for categorical grants on a project-by-project basis. Critics of this grantsmanship argued that the system created incentives for applicants to design local projects more in accordance with federal-agency objectives than with local needs. Formula funding eliminated the need for grantsmanship and made receipt of funds independent of the design of local programs. Besides formula distribution, the New Federalism sought to promote local autonomy by loosening the requirements that accompanied categorical grants. Local officials would

The El Paso experience described here is based on research, including interviews with city officials and analysis of city documents, conducted between November 1978 and April 1979 and reported more fully in Hudson (1979). Figures cited are from documents on file and the El Paso comptroller's reports.

work within broad federal guidelines, which gave them control of the specifics of programs. In general revenue-sharing, this flexibility was almost complete; in block-grant programs, there was flexibility within broad categories of funding.

This chapter describes the impact of New Federalism reforms on local autonomy in a single city: El Paso, Texas. Although an overall assessment of the impact of the New Federalism on political decentralization would require a much broader sample of municipalities, the intensive analysis of this single case is instructive because of the paradoxical impact that the New Federalism has had on El Paso. Instead of promoting local autonomy, the New Federalism grants—revenue sharing (GRS), community development (C-D), comprehensive employment and training (CETA), and counter-cyclical revenue-sharing—have helped to reduce city-government autonomy. Since the early 1970s, El Paso's dependence on federal funds as a source of revenue has increased dramatically, local officials have become politically dependent on continued high levels of federal funding, and requirements in the form of federal mandates affect local government activities more than ever before. The New Federalism has thus reduced rather than increased the city's independence from Washington. The analysis of this case suggests certain nonobvious hypotheses about the impact of New Federalism reforms, which may be applicable to other cities.

Dependence on Federal Revenue

Instead of loosening the ties between El Paso and the federal government, the New Federalism had the ironic effect of introducing the city to significant levels of federal funding. Prior to receiving its first revenue-sharing entitlement, El Paso received a very small amount of federal aid. Before 1966 federal aid was a miniscule factor, never more than 1 percent, in the city budget (U.S. Census Bureau 1964-1966). Even with the influx of funds for Great Society programs, federal aid never accounted for more than 5 percent of all city revenues. But with the introduction of the first GRS entitlements in the fiscal year 1973 budget, federal funds jumped from 2.4 percent of total revenue in FY 1972 to 19 percent in FY 1973. Between 1973 and 1976, federal funds comprised from one-fifth to one-fourth of the total budget (U.S. Census Bureau 1972-1977). New Federalism helped make the 1970s the decade of federal funds for El Paso.

Given its low participation in categorical programs before 1972, El Paso did not fit the model of a city constrained by stringent federal guidelines. Conservative political leaders throughout the 1960s had not sought federal funds because they wished to avoid the restrictions of federal guidelines and because they did not share the aims of Great Society programs. Given the marginality of grants in the local budget, categorical grants did not limit local autonomy. With the New Federalism, this passive, conservative posture was irrelevant to participation since funds were distributed automatically. The promotion of GRS by the conservative Nixon administration and the no-strings character of GRS also seems to have eased concerns about El Paso's participation. Even though El Paso's two conservative mayors between 1973 and 1976 continued to voice reservations about federal grants, federal funding increased rapidly.

The impact of the New Federalism on the city budget has been far from conservative. Between 1972 and 1976 the city's total budget grew from $46 million to $78 million; by 1978, the general fund budget—excluding capital project, airport, water, and sewer funds—alone was almost $100 million. Federal grants have accounted for 63 percent of the general fund budget growth since 1972. Table 8-1 demonstrates the growing importance of intergovernmental revenue (which is nearly exclusively federal revenue) for basic city operations in the 1970s. With the introduction of the New Federalism programs after 1972, the intergovernmental portion of city revenues expanded from 5 percent to nearly 50 percent. With such a high proportion of funds coming from the federal government, the local budget is quite sensitive to changes in federal policy. In 1978 when Congress failed to reauthorize countercyclical revenue-sharing, the city's fiscal 1979 budget, which the city council had already approved, was immediately thrown out of balance, and the city government was in technical violation of the city charter's balanced-budget requirement. Only a hasty sale of city-owned land and the cancellation of some capital improvements brought the budget in balance. Fiscally the city had come to depend on federal funds for a large proportion of its total budget, partly as a result of federal policy, which has made these funds easily available.

Table 8-1
Growing Importance of Intergovernmental Revenues in the El Paso General Fund, 1972-1978

Year	Percent Own Source Revenue	Percent Intergovernmental Revenue	Total Revenue (thousands)
1972	94.5	5.5	$27,137
1973	86.4	13.6	36,003
1974	83.8	16.2	40,524
1975	79.2	20.8	47,963
1976	74.1	25.9	55,301
1977	65.9	34.1	64,129
1978	53.2	46.8	96,617

Source: *El Paso Comptroller's Reports*, 1975-1978.

The local political environment now requires high levels of federal funding to support expanded basic services, tax stability, and the satisfaction of new citizen demands. Raising local revenues to cover the expansion of local government over the past seven years would be politically impossible. This is a situation about which local politicians are very aware. As one said, "If they [the federal government] pull the carpet out from under us, we're in for a long fall." Citizen demands for the benefits provided with federal funds (services and stable taxes) are a permanent part of local politics, and meeting them requires continued federal funding.

El Paso's dependence on federal revenues grows directly out of the flexibility allowed city officials to support basic city services with New Federalism grants. Inflation and the city's growth, reflected in a 33 percent population increase since 1970, are the primary sources of pressure on the city budget. The New Federalism programs have made funds available to support expanded basic services while allowing stable tax rates. There has been no effective tax increase since 1971; in fact the actual local tax burden has declined steadily since 1972, despite tremendous growth in spending. Every year since 1973, the city's basic operations have required an increasing proportion of intergovernmental revenue. Also nearly all capital spending in the 1970s was financed out of federal funds, allowing the city to avoid any bond issues between 1968 and 1979. For example, approximately $23 million to $25 million in capital improvements in 1977 were federally funded. New Federalism grants have been crucial for both basic capital improvements and basic city services.

Among the various New Federalism grants, CETA and countercyclical funds have been especially important for the expansion of services, and GRS and C-D funds have supported both capital projects and expanded services. The city's largest departments, police and fire, have used CETA funds to expand their personnel rosters incrementally. Each year new positions are created. Funded first out of CETA revenues, they are then supported with local revenues the second year as new CETA-funded positions are added. Countercyclical funds have been included in the general fund budget to support all basic services. In the early years, GRS funds were restricted to capital projects, which are one-time expenditures, but gradually large proportions have gone into the general fund; 70 percent of GRS entitlements 8 and 9 (1978) went to the general fund (table 8-2). C-D funds support both capital projects and basic services in those parts of the city designated as neighborhood strategy areas.

Since local politicians can offer new services and other improvements without raising taxes, they have been more willing than in the past to respond to citizen demands. Traditionally the city has not taken responsibility for improvements such as street paving, curbing, street lighting, and

Table 8-2
General Revenue-Sharing Entitlements, 1972-1978

Entitlement Period	Amount (thousands)	Percent Capital Shares	Percent Operating Shares
1. January 1972-June 1972	$ 2,712	n.a.	n.a.
2. July 1972-December 1972	2,602	n.a.	n.a.
3. January 1973-June 1973	3,118	80	20
4. July 1973-June 1974	6,254	92	8
5. July 1974-June 1975	6,080	100	0
6. July 1975-June 1976	6,826	72	28
7. July 1976-December 1976	3,411	37	63
8,9. January 1977-June 1978	10,811	30	70

Source: El Paso Office of Management and Budget.

drainage in El Paso's poor neighborhoods, especially the southside Mexican-American barrio. New Federalism funds, particularly C-D money, have been allocated for these purposes, with aldermen playing highly visible roles in announcing the allocations. Aldermen tend to peceive increased demands resulting from federal funds as citizens now come to expect such improvements in their neighborhoods. One alderman finds this typical of the C-D program: "It leads to citizens asking for more. . . . The other night at a C-D meeting a lady got up and said 'You fixed up this neighborhood, that neighborhood, when are you going to get around to *my* neighborhood.' You hear this constantly." Elderly citizens have also received new services as the result of federal grants. The Parks and Recreation director thinks that federally funded recreation centers have stimulated political organization among senior citizens, who now gather to discuss further demands to press upon government.

Experience with the New Federalism has helped to convince El Paso's political leaders of the advantages of federal funding for supporting new projects and programs with which they can identify themselves. El Paso's traditional reluctance to seek categorical grants seems to have evaporated in the last two years as the city administration has pursued grants aggressively. This shift in view can be seen in the attitudes of El Paso's aldermen who all see pursuit of federal revenue as a legitimate way to return federal tax revenue to El Paso's citizens. One self-styled conservative alderman argues, "As long as the feds are going to hand out money, there is no reason for the city to say no. It's our tax money and this is the only way we get some back." This desire to get El Paso's share of federal revenue led to the creation of a new grantsmanship office in 1978 to seek aid and to advise city departments on obtaining federal grants. Various aldermen have also promoted the creation of new city agencies funded with a mix of New Federalism, categorical, and local funds, from an Economic Development Office to an Arts and Humanities Office. The New Federalism seems to have helped bring grantsmanship to El Paso.

Diminished Local Autonomy

Local political dependence on federal revenues gives the federal government immense potential political leverage in the community. Since local officials cannot do without federal funds, they are likely to go along with conditions attached to them. Recently scholars have begun to give attention to general federal mandates applicable to New Federalism and categorical grants alike and their impact on local government (Lovell et al. 1979). In El Paso, officials perceive both procedural and substantive impacts of mandates on local actions, and sometimes even procedural requirements can have substantive impacts. For example, the police department found its traditional practice of informally reassigning officers to different divisions as work loads varied to be in potential violation of equal-employment-opportunity guidelines. Mindful of possible criticism from CETA auditors, the police chief decided to institute formal (and time-consuming) procedures for temporary transfers. Given mandates, local officials find the intervention of federal policy in their activities an everyday occurrence.

The New Federalism's impact has been to tie El Paso even more closely to Washington. Despite the flexibility of GRS and block grants, the presence of federal funds has carried with it federal guidelines and oversight by federal officials. More important, the New Federalism has affected the local political context as local elected officials have used the funds to satisfy their own constituencies. It is likely that local citizens in general, the poor, the elderly, and taxpayers, have benefited from federal aid; that aid has produced more-adequate levels of service but at the cost of some local autonomy. The El Paso case suggests that the New Federalism intended impact on decentralization may have been very different from what was expected.

To what extent is the El Paso experience with the New Federalism applicable to other cities and federal-local relations in general? Some obvious factors in the El Paso case that affected its response to the New Federalism may not be true of other cities. El Paso's low-level involvement in the federal grant system prior to 1973 made its reaction to formula funding very different from what may have been the case in other cities. Cities already dependent in the early 1970s on federal categorical funds may have found the greater flexibility of New Federalism, especially the consolidation of some categorical programs in CETA and C-D, a genuine factor in promoting local autonomy. Also El Paso's economic condition of a growing rather than a declining economic base makes it very different from many other cities, especially those in the Northeast. Some cities may find themselves dependent on federal revenues for economic reasons, no matter what form those funds take. For them, the flexibility of the New Federalism money may provide a measure of independence beyond what they would obtain if external support were in the form of categorical grants. Thus the impact of the New Federalism on federal-local relations depends to some extent on the pattern of distribution of categorical grants prior to 1973 and variations in economic conditions of local governments.

The New Federalism has not been the only federal policy affecting federal-local centralization in the 1970s. The federal government has provided larger amounts of aid to subsidiary governments than ever before, and this may be a centralizing factor no matter what the form of aid. Also the New Federalism revolution is incomplete in that much urban aid remains categorical in nature, continuing to tie cities to federal agencies through federal guidelines (ACIR 1977). In this regard, however, by introducing more cities to the advantages of federal funding, the New Federalism may have encouraged more cities to seek categorical aid aggressively, as occurred in El Paso.

In spite of these reservations, the New Federalism has probably been a key to diminished local autonomy throughout the federal system. By tying more cities to federal aid, formula funding may have significantly increased overall centralization (Stanfield 1978). The dispersion of federal aid to more cities also may have increased pressures on more congressional members to support high levels of urban aid. In addition, the discretion allowed local officials in New Federalism programs may promote political dependence regardless of previous experience with categorical funds and/or economic conditions. Local officials can use this discretion to pursue personal political goals and satisfy particular constituencies, making their own political careers dependent on federal aid. The New Federalism may have made federal funds, and thus the federal budget and federal policy, more relevant to local politics everywhere.

The El Paso case indicates that the impact of the New Federalism on local autonomy depends on how it affects overall local budget making and the political context in which budget decisions are made. If the New Federalism has helped to make federal funding policy a factor in all taxing and spending decisions, as seems to be the case in El Paso, it can hardly be regarded as having promoted local independence from Washington. More studies taking a wide view of the overall impact of the New Federalism on local politics are needed before we can determine if it has helped reverse the twentieth-century trend toward governmental centralization in America.

References

Advisory Commission on Intergovernmental Relations. 1977. *Block Grants: A Comparative Analysis*. Washington, D.C.: Government Printing Office.

Caputo, D.A., and Cole, R.L. 1974. *Urban Politics and Decentralization*. Lexington, Mass.: Lexington Books, D.C. Heath and Co.

Heller, Walter. 1968. "A Sympathetic Reappraisal of Revenue Sharing." In Harvey S. Perloff and Richard P. Nathan, eds., *Revenue-sharing and the City*. Baltimore, Md.: Johns Hopkins Press.

Hudson, William E. 1979. "Local Government Dependence on Federal Revenues: The El Paso Experience." Paper presented to the Southwestern Political Science Association, 28 March.

Lovell, Catherine H. et al. 1979. *Federal and State Mandates on Local Governments: An Exploration of Issues and Impacts*. Riverside, Calif.: Graduate School of Administration, University of California.

Nathan, Richard. 1975. *The Plot That Failed: Nixon and the Administrative Presidency*. New York: Wiley.

Nathan, Richard, and Adams, Charles. 1977. *Revenue-sharing: The Second Round*. Washington, D.C.: Brookings Institution.

Stanfield, Rochelle L. 1978. "Federal Aid for the Cities—Is It a Mixed Blessing." *National Journal* 22:866-872.

Thompson, Richard A. 1973. *Revenue-sharing: A New Era in Federalism?* Washington, D.C.: Revenue-sharing Advisory Service.

U.S. Bureau of the Census. 1964-1978. *City Government Finances*. Washington, D.C.: Government Printing Office.

9

Block Grants and Urban Policies: Implementation and Impact

E. Terrence Jones

Much of the federal government's domestic-policy process involves attempts to get state and local jurisdictions to pursue national goals. In a complex society with dispersed power, no single unit of government contains within itself the wherewithal to accomplish its objectives. Other entities must be incorporated in the policy's implementation in order to achieve the desired impact. As a result, the national government has employed an enormous array of carrots and sticks in an effort to get subnational units to carry out federal policy.

In order to help understand the implications of this situation for designing intergovernmental aid programs, let us imagine a cancer ward with hundreds of patients. All are suspected of having cancer, although a few might have been misdiagnosed, but the type and degree of growth vary considerably from one case to the next. Some financial resources are available for treating the ill, but the dollars are not infinite.

What would be the best treatment policy in such a situation? How much money should be allocated to each case? Should the most curable receive the highest priority? Whatever the allocation pattern, how should the money be spent? What kind of treatment should be applied to each patient, who should make the treatment selection, and how should the decision—once made—be assessed? Given a fixed allocation, should the patient determine his or her own treatment, or should some experts devise treatment strategies for each type of patient?

Most American urban areas do have certain cancers, and federal policy makers have debated a wide range of treatment policies and attempted several of them. In the 1970s, the preferred treatment for many urban ills—such as inadequate housing, physical blight, and unemployment—was the block-grant program (Mirengoff and Rindler 1978; Nathan et al. 1977; Van Horn 1979). The two most prominent block-grant programs have been authorized by the Comprehensive Employment and Training Act of 1973 and the Housing and Community Development Act of 1974. Within each policy area, eligible jurisdictions are defined, measures of need are established, funds are allocated on the basis of the need indicators, and local officials ostensibly have substantial discretion in spending the block grant allocation.

In terms of the cancer-ward metaphor, the facility's operators provide the funds, determine the allocations among patients, and set the general goals. The directors allow patients much latitude in devising their treatments, although they require that the patients prepare plans before receiving the funds and submit performance reports after spending their allocations.

When cast in a medical analogy, in the block-grants situation, allowing the patient to serve as the controlling intermediary between national dollar input and nationally established goals appears a rather shaky strategy. Although patients' control over their own bodies sounds like an excellent principle, patients differ enormously in their ability to translate the cancer ward's financial resources into effective outcomes. The patients may believe in their own policies and may want to supervise their own treatment, but their cancers are not likely to be ameliorated.

So, too, urban jurisdictions may stand behind their locally devised community-development or manpower policies and be proud about running their own programs, but one may be decidedly suspicious about their ability to translate federally provided funds into federally established goals. Local jurisdictions vary considerably in the ways in which they react to an infusion of federal funds (Dommel et al. 1978; Lieske 1978; Ripley et al. 1978; Rosenfeld 1979; Van Horn 1978). Although one can hope that locally designed policies adapted to the particular situation within each jurisdiction will produce noticeable movement toward national goals, little empirical evidence supports such optimism. Local polities are quite diverse, and this diversity sends block-grant dollars down many channels. Where these channels lead is largely unknown to those doing the diverting and, in many cases, the initial diversion is—from the standpoint of the local actors—sufficient unto itself.

This chapter identifies several key differences among block-grant recipient jurisdictions that can and often do have a significant effect on how federal-aid funds are spent. These differences will be illustrated with the Community Development Block Grant (CDBG) and the Comprehensive and Employment Training Act (CETA) programs in the city of St. Louis, a declining central city, and St. Louis County, a large suburban county. The study period extends from the initial receipt of block-grant dollars in 1974 and 1975 to late 1979.

Local jurisdictions have different starting points. When the first block-grant dollars arrived, not every locality was in the same place. Some were deeply involved in community-development and manpower policies, others had modest efforts, and a small remainder had virtually no programs. Since where you go depends in part on where you are, these diverse starting points influenced the direction of local CDBG and CETA programs.

When the CDBG allocations began in 1975, the city of St. Louis had major urban renewal and Model Cities projects, which had their own bureaucratic and political dynamics. Given these projects' existing momentum and the need to commit CDBG funds quickly, these two activities were almost inevitable recipients of over half of the initial CDBG budget.

Unlike the city, St. Louis County had little experience with the previous urban categorical grants. The CDBG funds represented new money, and the moderate-to-conservative Republican administration was not about to squander all or most of the funds on programs targeted to the county's poorest groups. Low- and moderate-income voters were not part of the Republican winning electoral coalition, and overtly catering to the poor was perceived as upsetting to traditional GOP voters. Moreover, the county, which had litle familiarity with managing urban renewal or providing social services, turned to what were more traditional activities such as storm water control, street improvements, and park development. Indeed the county had no established bureaucracy for delivering social services so that in the short run it could not emphasize that option.

Local jurisdictions have different grant-processing capacities. When given the opportunity to spend additional millions of dollars, some polities can respond faster than others (Bardach 1977; Pressman and Wildavsky 1973; Van Meter and Van Horn 1975). Jurisdictions with existing community-development or manpower agencies and with sophisticated personnel and financial-management systems can plan, implement, and monitor CDBG and CETA expenditures more quickly than can those without such capabilities.

Both the city of St. Louis and St. Louis County lacked some grant-processing capacity and, as a result, initially had relatively slow rates of spending. CDBG and CETA funds. In both jurisdictions, new agencies had to be formed, personnel classifications had to be established and then filled, and financial procedures had to be developed and implemented. Both the city and the county were somewhat overwhelmed by the sheer size of the block-grant dollars—almost $200 million in the first four years—and, even after this period, their capacity is still not fully adequate.

In some instances, the situation has been exacerbated by a lack of cooperation between the existing centralized management operations, personnel and finance, and the new block-grant agencies. Commonly the personnel and financial offices are tradition-laden and reluctant to respond expediiously to the new agencies' expanded and different needs. Moreover, the old personnel and financial entities seldom received any additional funding to support the increased demand on their resources. They had no incentive to cooperate with the new agencies. The result in both the city and the county has been a mix of less-than-friendly bargaining between the new and old policy systems and, when this was not fully effective, the establishment of miniature but potentially duplicative personnel and finance processes within the block-grant agencies.

Local jurisdictions have different bureaucratic styles. How an organization operates affects the programs it produces. This truism is best expressed in the St. Louis situation by the different informal hiring patterns used by the block-grant agencies. The city's Community Development Agency is an outgrowth of the older planning agency. Most of its key staff members have planning backgrounds and, as the agency has grown, the planners have reproduced themselves. Not surprisingly, the agency's efforts frequently reflect a strong physical planning mentality (Altshuler 1965; Rabinovitz 1969). There is an emphasis on grand redevelopment strategies, with visually exciting physical improvements seen as the key independent variables that will leverage massive urban redevelopment. Much less attention has been given to social factors, either as causes or effects.

The city's manpower operation (St. Louis Agency on Training and Employment, or SLATE) started after CETA was passed in 1973. From the beginning, its staff has had a substantial number of education and social-work professionals. The result is an agency that is very client-oriented but operates on an individualistic, one-case-at-a-time basis. Staff members have not had strong backgrounds in manpower planning or, until very recently, management processes. SLATE thus generally impresses one as an agency that cares very much about the unemployed but is very uncertain about where it is going or, for that matter, where it has been.

Local jurisdictions have different kinds of chief elected executives. Mayors can differ in many ways, and these qualities will affect their approach to block-grant programs. One that merits special attention, however, is future political ambitions. As other analysts have noted (Mayhew 1974), tomorrow's career aspirations can do a lot to help explain today's political behavior.

In the city of St. Louis, the current mayor was first elected in 1977 and, by his own frank admission, wants to be reelected in 1981. A key element in his electoral coalition has been the financial support of the city's corporate leadership. This influential civic elite supports the notion that a strong city begins with a revitalized downtown. Accordingly when neighborhood and downtown interests conflict in allocating CDBG funds, the mayor has tended to back the downtown approach and opt for economic development over residential rehabilitation.

In St. Louis County, the incumbent Republican county supervisor was reelected to a four-year term by a healthy margin in 1978. In 1980 he set his eyes on running against Thomas Eagleton for U.S. senator, using a low-tax, low-service campaign theme with an anti-Washington motif. Accordingly at times he seemed embarrassed by even accepting CDBG and CETA funds and has insisted that they be used exclusively for preservation purposes: rebuilding storm water systems, repairing streets, or rehabilitating owner-occupied single-family houses.

As this expenditure trend continued through the county's first four CDBG years, the Department of Housing and Urban Development (HUD) became increasingly concerned that the county was not taking sufficient care to use CDBG funds to benefit low- and moderate-income families and asked the county to make some modest changes in its fifth-year application. What was apparently intended by HUD to be a small-scale bargaining session was seen by the county supervisor as a prime opportunity to run against an oppressive Washington bureaucracy out to destroy local autonomy. He refused to bargain, escalated the conflict, and told HUD either to accept the original fifth-year application or else to go to court. Painted into a corner, HUD chose adjudication and was thereby cast to play the villain in the supervisor's 1980 campaign. Subsequently a reassessment of its legal position and, one suspects, some pressure from Senator Eagleton and the White House combined to cause HUD to negotiate an out-of-court settlement, which put little pressure on the county to change its originally planned CDBG allocations.

Local jurisdictions have different types of legislatures. Neither the CDBG nor the CETA programs require any substantial local legislative involvement. Although the councils can and do enact ordinances approving the applications, there is no requirement that they play any role in either formulating or implementing block-grant programs. Since most local legislators are part-time and since professional legislative staff is minimal, it took some time for most councils to become fully aware of the growing importance of block-grant dollars in local policy making.

Once legislatures began to pay attention to the CDBG and CETA millions, what they did about it depended largely on their previous style and role. In the city of St. Louis, the board of aldermen is a classic ward-based, division-of-the-spoils legislature with a long tradition of log-rolling and pork-barreling. As the block-grant programs became a more familiar part of the urban budget, their involvement contributed to a greater geographical dispersal of funds and increased support for more divisible projects. It is politically better to give one hundred grants of $5,000 each than award one grant of $500,000. In 1978, for example, each of the city's 126 census tracts received at least $25,000 in CDBG funds.

In St. Louis County, on the other hand, the council is small (seven members compared to the city's twenty-eight), has little power compared to the county supervisor, and operates in an atmosphere that often regards open bargaining as an urban pollutant. Consequently the county council has had virtually no impact on CDBG and CETA allocations.

It is unreasonable to expect every local jurisdiction to march to the same drumbeat toward identical goals. Any block-grant allocation with broadly defined ends enters a local polity's ongoing stream. Since the stream has its own momentum, which, in turn, is the product of many local factors, it is much more likely that the block-grant dollars will be swept along with the prevailing current than that the federal grant will cause a noticeable change in the stream. Although there may be a rare jurisdiction where a certain block-grant program arrived at a very propitious moment and thereby contributed to a substantial policy shift, from a more realistic viewpoint the most that block grants can do is to induce modest alterations in the stream's direction and flow.

Moreover, the extent of these changes differs from one city to the next. Perhaps a battalion of urban-politics specialists could review each jurisdiction's CDBG and CETA applications annually to determine if the proposed programs would do all that could be accomplished given the nature of the local polity. The political science doctors would examine each patient's treatment plan to see if—for that type of case—the program promised to make reasonable progress toward alleviating the cancer. Cases with high capacities (such as sophisticated management systems) or favorable conditions (perhaps a mayor elected by a low-income coalition) would be expected to accomplish more than cases with low capacities (such as understaffed or poorly developed bureaucracies) or unfavorable conditions (a conservative mayor). Such an approach would not ask for more from a jurisdiction than it could reasonably be expected to deliver.

Although such an approach tailors expectations about tomorrow to assessments of today, it also has flaws. First, knowledge about local polities is extremely uneven. It varies considerably from city to city, from year to year, and from expert to expert, so it would be impossible to produce consistently top-quality assessments. Second, federal law and federal guidelines are based on equal-treatment principles. How would one legally apply tougher standards to one jurisdiction than to another on the grounds that the latter area's political situation prevented it from making any more progress toward national goals?

The dilemma is real. Maintaining local autonomy and achieving national goals are far from mutually compatible. For the present, it appears, one must lean toward accepting Lowi's (1979, pp. 195-196) conclusion:

> Since the national government is precisely a national government, and since each city is special, a federal policy oriented toward cities as such can be general only if it is vague. But if these programs make federal funds available without any criteria they are merely an open invitation to scramble. . . . Under these circumstances federal aid enables local elites to reinforce local patterns and practices.

References

Altschuler, Alan. 1965. *The City Planning Process*. Ithaca, N.Y.: Cornell University Press.

Bardach, Eugene. 1977. *The Implementation Game*. Cambridge, Mass.: MIT Press.

Dommel, Paul R. et al. 1978. *Decentralizing Community Development*. Washington, D.C.: Department of Housing and Urban Development.

Lieske, Joel A. 1978. "Manpower and the New Federalism: The Transition to CETA." *Publius* 8:129-151.

Lowi, Theodore J. 1979. *The End of Liberalism*. 2d ed. New York: W.W. Norton.

Mayhew, David R. 1974. *The Electoral Connection*. New Haven, Conn.: Yale University Press.

Mirengoff, William, and Rindler, Lester. 1978. *CETA: Manpower Programs under Local Control*. Washington, D.C.: Natural Academy of Sciences.

Nathan, Richard P. et al. 1977. *Block Grants for Community Development*. Washington, D.C.: Government Printing Office.

Pressman, Jeffrey L., and Wildavsky, Aaron. 1973. *Implementation*. Berkeley: University of California Press.

Rabinovitz, Francine. 1969. *City Politics and Planning*. New York: Atherton.

Ripley, Randall B. et al. 1978. *CETA Prime Sponsor Management Decisions and Program Goal Achievement*. Washington, D.C.: Department of Labor.

Rosenfeld, Raymond A. 1979. "Local Implementation Decisions for Community Development Block Grants." *Public Administration Review* 39:448-457.

Van Horn, Carl E. 1978. "Implementing CETA: The Federal Role." *Policy Analysis* 4:159-183.

_____ . 1979. "Evaluating the New Federalism: National Goals and Local Implementors." *Public Administration Review* 39:17-22.

Van Meter, Donald S., and Van Horn, Carl E. 1975. "The Policy Implementation Process: A Conceptual Framework." *Administration and Society* 6:445-488.

10 Desegregation Becomes Gentrification

Edmund Beard and
Peter DiToro

Boston's South End is an inner-city neighborhood barely a mile from the downtown financial and commercial center and abutting the busy Prudential Center complex along Boylston Street. The land itself was created as part of Boston's massive land-fill operations of the nineteenth century, which also created the nearby, and now quite elegant, Back Bay. The South End developed quickly after 1830. Soon after the Civil War a number of important churches were built there, and it became a fashionable locale for the upper middle class.

Much of the South End's housing stock consists of gracious bow front, brick town houses built in the mid-nineteenth century for that middle- or upper-income public. Yet the South End's prime was short-lived. During the last third of the nineteenth century the area began to decline as competition from the Back Bay along Commonwealth Avenue and Beacon and Newbury streets, as well as from Brookline and the streetcar suburbs of Allston, Jamaica Plain, and Dorchester, which were annexed to Boston in the 1870s, took its toll. When the horse-drawn streetcar system was extended, a growing middle class was able to reach new, affordable, two- or three-family free-standing houses with modest lawns in those last areas (City of Boston 1978).

Other factors, including the 1873 real-estate panic, hurt the South End. Within a few years many of the larger houses had been transformed into rooming houses and tenements. Soon the area became a recognized initial settling place for immigrants, a role that persisted when those immigrants began coming from the Caribbean and the American South rather than from Europe. Because of this phenomenon, the South End over the years evolved into the most heterogeneous, ethnically diverse neighborhood in Boston. Yet as the neighborhood's population became more diverse, it also shrank. In 1910 the South End held 76,000 people. By 1940 that figure had fallen to 51,000 and by 1966 to only 26,000. Nearly 50 percent of those 26,000 persons were nonwhite.

Although half of the residential buildings and 10 percent of the total housing units were owner-occupied in the early 1960s, the South End by then had fallen into very poor shape. In 1960, for example, "53.9% of the housing units were substandard and 10.4% of the units vacant. . . . The

South End [had] 923 licensed lodging houses, 116 licensed bars and liquor stores and a good portion of Boston's skid row" (Whittlesey 1969, p. 1).

With the neighborhood's deterioration and with its increasing image as one of the homes first of Boston's black and later of its Hispanic communities had also come a decline in municipal services. Yet the South End's location was potentially a major plus. That same highly visible location made the South End of 1960 a considerable embarrassment to city officials. Beginning in 1960 the South End was placed high in Boston's urban-renewal plans.

The resulting Boston Redevelopment Authority (BRA) 1964 Urban Renewal Plan called for the rehabilitation of 75 percent of the residential buildings in a 616-acre area. As one careful study of the original BRA efforts pointed out, "The plan emphasizes residential rehabilitation. . . . The renewal plan suggests that this would be carried out for the benefit of South End residents who choose to remain in the area. As a substantial portion of these residents are low-income families and persons, residential rehabilitation which permits rents which low-income families and persons can afford is a prerequisite for the success of the plan" (Whittlesey 1969, pp. 5-6).

Money was also spent on the area's infrastructure to improve streets, sidewalks, sewer and water lines, lighting, and parks. These developments, combined with the quality of the original houses and the area's central location, rapidly made the South End very attractive to young white professionals looking for a first home or moving back to the city, to a much smaller number of black professionals in similar circumstances, and to real-estate speculators attempting to profit from both groups' interest.

The influx of these new groups over the past two decades has been striking. Indeed the area is now substantially gentrified. As one recent review concluded, in a mixture of description and exhortation, "The renewal programs in Charlestown or the South End have succeeded in attracting such a flood of middle and higher income households that existing residents who cannot afford the rising rents have been displaced. If future public policy is to be effective, the focus must remain on people, not structures; houses and neighborhoods only reflect the well-being of the households themselves" (BRA and BUO 1975, p. 262).

The Policy

Section 8 of the Housing and Community Development Act of 1974 established what has come to be known as the spatial-deconcentration principle, the purpose of which was to disperse urban-area federal housing subsidies and thereby lessen local housing authorities' (that is, mayors') control over economic and racial patterns in assisted housing. Specifically its intent was to end federal subsidy of local segregation in public housing. This was to be accomplished by restricting the power of local authorities to concentrate federal monies—and therefore persons assisted by federal monies—in any one place while correspondingly increasing the role of the Department of Housing and Urban Development (HUD) in local site selection. Beyond reduction of locally sanctioned, federally subsidized segregation, intended results included the provision of good-quality, mixed housing to low-income groups. In particular the new law sought to avoid such patterns as the public-housing system operated by the Chicago Housing Authority in the 1960s, which was found to be racially segregated; four overwhelmingly white projects were located in white neighborhoods, while 99.5 percent of the remaining family units were located in black neighborhoods with 99 percent of those units occupied by black tenants (*Hills* v. *Gautreaux* 1976).

Clustered together, poorer households were also expected to be less able to claim and, more importantly, actually obtain decent city services, quality schools, and adequate police protection than if they were combined with higher-income, more-visible households with greater political influence and experience (BRA and BUO 1975, pp. 226-227). Thus residential integration through deconcentration of lower-income groups from central cities was expected to produce both racial integration and political efficacy. In the words of another U.S. district court, "Congress apparently decided that this was part of the solution to the crisis facing our urban communities" (*City of Hartford* v. *Hills* 1976).

Section 8 in the South End: The Unintended Consequences

Inquilinos Boriquas en Accion (IBA) (Puerto Rican Tenants in Action, formerly known as ETC, or Emergency Tenants Council) was organized in the 1960s as a response to the initiatives of the Boston Redevelopment Authority. Fearing displacement, campaigners wearing buttons announcing "no nos mudaremos de la parcela 19" [We will not move from parcel 19] canvassed the neighborhood. They incorporated their organization in August 1968.

After considerable political negotiation, ETC was given permission and funding in the early 1970s for the rehabilitation of community structures. The result was the initiation of the largest resident-controlled housing construction program to date in the United States. Significantly ETC's goal was the prevention of resident displacement through a comprehensive plan that included elderly and family housing, social facilities and services, and commercial activity, all to be controlled by the residents.

Currently IBA is an umbrella organization covering the activities of its various components. The development arm is known as ETC Development

Corporation and is a wholly owned subsidiary of IBA. IBA-ETC controls 657 units of South End housing and provides as well a broad range of cultural and social services, including day care, recreational services, cultural programs, a real-estate brokerage service, and the coordination of contiguous commercial development. Through its organizational structure, IBA guarantees resident control. Three hundred forty paying members elect a residents-only board of directors. Resident organizations have direct access to the IBA hierarchy. IBA is also staffed predominantly by Hispanic personnel.

Viviendas la Victoria I (Victory Housing I) is the heart of IBA's operation. It consists of fifty-four two-family, town-house-style structures, one midrise, multiunit building, and six thousand square feet of community space. The midrise structure faces Plaza Betances, a Puerto Rican-style plaza that is the symbolic center of the Hispanic community. The project was completed in 1976 and serves low- and moderate-income residents.

Viviendas la Victoria II is an extension of IBA's earlier efforts. The original plan was to build 207 new units, including more town houses and an extension of the Plaza Betances. The town houses were to fill in the area contiguous to Vivendas la Victoria I and create a cultural and architectural whole. Sources of seed money or technical assistance include the United Catholic Conference Campaign for Human Development, the Episcopal City Mission, and the Greater Boston Community Development Corporation. Financing has been arranged through the Department of Housing and Urban Development 221(d)(4) mortgage guarantee and Section 8 subsidy programs. Amenities are to include disposals, community space at the multistory building, laundries, private yards for the town houses, parking facilities, gardens, tot lots, and extensive landscaping.

Richard Hall of the BRA has said of IBA's earlier effort, "It's very much a model community. Tenant management is the key." Kenneth Salk of HUD's Boston office added, "They've made the whole South End more viable. I'd rate them in the top one percent [of such housing developers]." IBA's architect has been commended by the Boston Society of Architects for his design of Viviendas la Victoria I. In 1978 IBA was the only community-based housing sponsor in Massachusetts to receive a grant from HUD for commercial and social-service development. An Hispanic member of the Massachusetts Commission against Discrimination has commented, "It's enabled the Hispanic community to survive and prosper in the place where Hispanics first sank their roots in Boston. IBA is a mecca in the South End. It's maintained the diversity of income and ethnic origin that people move to the South End to be close to." (*Boston Globe*, 8 February 1979). In 1973-1974 IBA also took over the management of, and successfully turned around, a struggling BHA project on West Newton Street in the South End.

However, a group of South End residents, organized as the Committee for an Open Review Process and consisting mainly of white-collar professionals, have petitioned the federal district court for a preliminary restraining order to prevent the demolition necessary for IBA to proceed on the 207 new units and for permanent injunctions stopping HUD and the BRA from funding the project. (Four years ago essentially the same group, then calling itself the Committee for a Balanced South End, tried to stop Viviendas la Victoria I but failed.)

The committee argues that demolition of eight houses planned by IBA as part of Viviendas la Victoria II violates historical-preservation statutes. The South End is a federally registered National Historical District. Any expenditure of federal funds that will affect an historical district requires a special environmental clearance, which HUD and the BRA had not acquired. However, the Committee for an Open Review Process admits that the historical-preservation issue is simply a preliminary feint. The basic argument the plaintiffs make is that this project would create "an undue concentration of assisted persons" under the Housing and Community Development Act's Section 8. As one of them puts it, "Congressional law is very clear on the concentration of low income people. The reason projects like this fail is people are concentrated who are incapable of capital formation."

The federal district court recently granted a preliminary restraining order preventing any demolition of the eight houses involved until HUD and BRA received the proper special environmental clearance (*Aertsen* v. *Landrieu*). To date this has not been completed, although it is in the process. IBA, however, has reworked its plans in order to preserve the shells and outer appearance of the eight houses. IBA estimates that an additional $500,000 will be required for structural reinforcement of the houses. Furthermore, plans for several six-bedroom apartments for large or extended families have had to be eliminated as infeasible within the confines of the existing houses. Still, IBA has made the adjustments and is prepared to proceed.

As of this writing the court had not ruled on the "undue concentration of low income people" issue, however, and that matter remains alive. No specific date had been set for the ruling. Until then IBA's plans are in limbo. HUD has remained firmly committed to the subsidies agreed upon. But until the court acts, IBA estimates that it is losing $3,000 a day in added costs caused by the delay. Since HUD has also decided not to renegotiate the agreement to cover IBA's unexpected cost increases, the $3,000 a day must come out of the project as designed. The result is that monies marked for communal, recreational, and commercial spaces, as well as for added amenities in the apartments, have been redirected to meet the new costs. IBA had hoped that construction could begin in the summer of 1980. However, in other situations, expensive delays have resulted in the cancellation of projects.

Thus a law originally intended to avoid racial segregation by local housing authorities, to stop undue concentrations of lower-income persons,
presumably against their wishes or best interests, by promoting "greater
choice of housing opportunities," is being used by a white professional
group to further the process of gentrification and in opposition to a successful, proven, community-originated, primarily Hispanic tenants'
organization. Of course HUD regulations do attempt "to avoid encouraging projects located in substantially racially mixed areas" (37 F.R. 204,
1972), but, again presumably, not to prevent an existing community from
preserving and improving itself.

Phil Bradley, the head of the ETC, has pointed out that a BRA study
completed in 1965 showed that 90 percent of the South End's population
had incomes falling within the eligibility cutoff for public housing so that
any argument that HUD, BRA, and IBA are creating an undue concentration of poor people, who were not there before, is false. Bradley, admittedly
an interested party, calls the opposition to IBA "racist and classist; the issue
is not historical preservation but race and poor people."

The Lessons

The spatial-deconcentration principle as embodied in Section 8 of the Housing and Community Development Act of 1974 was designed to end at least
one form of federally subsidized local patterns of segregation, to increase
the capacity of poor households to secure adequate municipal services by
associating them with more influential, higher-income neighbors, and to
begin to resolve other problems of urban blight attributed to a critical-mass
effect such as property abandonment and increased crime rates.

No doubt there were other goals and perceptions, such as that suburban
jobs would be made more accessible to low-income workers or, more
subtly, that attendance at economically integrated schools would be better
somehow for poor children just as daily personal interaction between their
parents and middle-class neighbors would be for the parents (Downs 1973).
The black activist Jesse Jackson, for example, has described the premise
behind similar white-initiated integration plans as that "we are inferior and
only by sitting next to white people, having white teachers, can we be
somebody" (BRA and BUO 1975, p. 217).

None of the conscious, admitted goals of spatial deconcentration were
to penalize a poor community trying to rehabilitate its housing or build
itself new housing. There may have been a racial or class suspicion that poor
people would be improved by proximity to middle-class behavior and
values, but there was no overtly expressed opposition to low-income
neighborhood self-help through better housing. The sponsors of spatial

deconcentration seem clearly not to have trusted the altruistic motives of local housing authorities. Yet they also seem to have been blind to the possibility that low-income areas might themselves use HUD subsidies for their own benefit instead of waiting passively for local elected or appointed officials to act, whether supportively or not.

The implementation literature has often ignored the importance of carefully chosen statutory language while focusing on local conditions, actors, and perspectives (Sabatier and Mazmanian 1980). This brief study indicates again the risks of unexamined legislative assumptions. The spatial-deconcentration principle was intended to protect and promote poor, minority populations. Yet in the South End of Boston, it is being used for opposite ends, at least in the eyes of the affected Hispanic population. To them, concentration in new or rehabilitated, self-managed, subsidized housing provides good-quality housing and offers social, cultural, and political advantages that otherwise would be lost. The congressional authors of the Housing and Community Development Act sought to protect minorities against segregation-minded local authorities. What they did in Boston was give a tool to middle-class whites who want neighbors like themselves but in a formerly Hispanic neighborhood.

The formal language of Section 8 seems to favor the Committee for an Open Review Process and to jeopardize IBA's plans for Viviendas la Victoria II. Whether the federal courts will look beyond that language and determine that the congressional intention was not to penalize groups like IBA remains to be seen. However, Congress would have improved IBA's chances if it had not taken such a narrow view of how to ensure better low-income housing.

This is not only an interesting political fight; it is also a classic case study of the unintended consequences of policy directives, in this case the failure of congressional and HUD planners to foresee the merits of some kinds of concentrations of lower-income persons. It raises interesting questions about the long-term effects of maintaining cultural, class (and potentially political) power bases, the meaning of mixed housing, and the politics of gentrification. In the short run, if Boston's Hispanic community is permitted to build any more subsidized housing where it lives in the South End, that housing is going to be smaller, consist of fewer units, and be substantially more costly than it might have been.

References

Aertsen v. *Landrieu.* 78-3271-6 (D. Mass.).

Boston Redevelopment Authority and Boston Urban Observatory. 1975. *Housing Policy Considerations for a Central City in a Metropolitan Contest: Boston, Mass.* Boston: BRA-BUO.

City of Boston. 1978. Office of Program Development. *Boston's Triple Deckers*.

City of Hartford v. *Hills*. 1976. 408 F. Supp. 889 (D. Conn.).

Downs, Anthony. 1973. *Opening Up the Suburbs*. New Haven: Yale University Press.

Hills v. *Gautreaux*. 1976. 425 U.S. 284.

Sabatier, Paul, and Mazmanian, Daniel. 1980. "The Implementation of Public Policy: A Framework of Analysis." *Policy Studies Journal* 8:538-560.

Whittlesey, Robert B. 1969. *The South End Row House and Its Rehabilitation for Low Income Residents*. Boston: South End Community Development.

Part III
Feedback of Policy Impact

Rarely do the consequences of public policies turn out exactly as intended. When the consequences are eventually discovered, it is almost always necessary to make corrective adjustments in the continuing implementation of the policy or to revise the basic policy statement itself in order to achieve the desired results. Occasionally it may even be necessary to abandon a policy altogether and try a completely new approach. The three chapters in this part illustrate each of these possibilities. Lester Milbrath focuses on water-quality planning in the Niagara Frontier under federal water-quality legislation. He discusses traditional methods of citizen involvement and shows how a survey of a public that feels the impact of such policies can increase the representation of citizen views and how such a mechanism can affect policy change. Gillian Dean presents methods for examining impact and feedback dynamics through the study of the reciprocal effects of state divorce policy and divorce rates. Nicholas Peroff describes a policy impact that was not only unintended but actually disastrous. The Menominee Termination Act of 1954 was designed to provide full assimilation of this Indian tribe. When the enormity of the negative social consequences became apparent, the policy was, in effect, reserved with the repeal of the 1954 legislation and enactment of the Menominee Restoration Act of 1973.

11 Incorporating the Views of the Uninterested but Impacted Public in Environmental Planning

Lester W. Milbrath

In recent years the federal government has mandated citizen participation in environmental planning. This mandate is particularly clear and forceful for the comprehensive water-quality plans recently developed in many regions of the country under Section 208 of the Water Quality Amendments of 1972. The federal Environmental Protection Agency, in its sponsorship and oversight of these so-called 208 plans, has strongly supported citizen participation in the development of these plans.

The intent of Congress in mandating citizen participation in water-quality planning has not been clear, yet it can be surmised that Congress had several motives in mind. First, it wanted plans to be developed that could be implemented in the light of local needs and that would take into account local political realities. Second, Congress recognized that making environmental plans is clearly part of the public's business. As such, the public must be able to have an important role in the development of environmental plans. Third, environmental plans nearly always involve important trade-offs. If those trade-offs are to be evaluated accurately, it is important that the public have an opportunity to express its values.

Methods for Citizen Participation

Specific methods for implementing citizen participation in planning were not elaborated by Congress and have been a continuing matter of experimentation and debate within federal agencies as well as by those publics that interact with environmental planners ("Symposium" 1976; Stewart 1974; USEPA 1976). My own observation suggests that thinking about citizen participation in most governmental and planning agencies has been naive and unimaginative. The programs, by and large, have failed to meet their objectives.

The traditional method for incorporating citizen input into environmental planning has been to set up citizen committees that interact with planners and with the public officials who supervise the activities of planners. Most of these committees are appointed by the planners or officials themselves rather than being self-selected or elected by the public. They involve only a tiny fraction of the general public. In most cases they are used implicitly or explicitly to co-opt certain interest groups. Careful planners or public officials give a great deal of consideration to the make-up of citizen committees to make sure that they interfere as little as possible with the planning task.

Committee participation often is supplemented by public hearings, usually held at the stage of presentation of alternative plans. Hearings are used routinely in many states without much consideration being given to their effectiveness for making wise public policy. Citizens also may transmit oral and written messages to planners and public officials any time they choose, but this channel of influence seems to be used infrequently.

Deficiencies of Citizen Participation

These methods of citizen representation in environmental planning suffer some serious deficiencies. The greatest is that citizen committees, even if they are supplemented by hearings, are by no means representative. Only a few citizens, most of them with a special interest to protect or promote, are likely to join committee activities. A tiny fraction of people participate out of a sense of citizen duty or because of a general interest in making a better environment. The number of citizens involved in typical planning committees will be less than 0.1 percent of the adult population. In a local 208 planning operation on the Niagara Frontier, a maximum of two hundred people, 0.01 percent of the public, became involved in one way or another in the development of the water-quality plan. If a thousand people could be brought to a public hearing (a highly unlikely prospect), they still would constitute less than 0.1 percent of the public in this two-county region. Furthermore these people would by no means be representative of the public view in the two counties. It also is clear that only a tiny fraction of the thousand people at the hearing could be given an opportunity to speak.

Most people are totally oblivious to 208 water-quality-planning efforts. Despite extensive efforts by the planning staff to get media coverage, 74 percent of the public in the two-county region reported in our first wave of interviews that they had never heard of the water-quality plan. When we reinterviewed the sample eighteen months later, 63 percent still reported that they could not recall any media coverage despite the fact that their consciousness very likely had been raised by our hour-long interview on the planning effort. When hearings were held in the auditorium of the county library to present the plan to the public, approximately forty people attended.

If one deducts from that total the number of public officials and planning staff who were present, the number of ordinary citizens in attendance was only about twenty (out of a total population of 1.2 million).

A second deficiency of traditional methods of citizen participation in environmental planning is that it is extremely difficult to sustain interest and active participation over several months. On the Niagara Frontier, for example, the Citizens' Advisory Committee spent considerable time in discussing the proper role of the committee and in trying to decide whether the committee had any role to play at all. Halfway through the planning process, the committee simply stopped meeting and died because of an inability to develop a proper role or to sustain interest.

Media attention to the planning effort, or to citizen participation in the effort, has provided little or no supplement to citizen participation effectiveness. For the most part media attention has been scanty or nonexistent despite the efforts of the 208 project staff to stimulate their interest and attention. The media gatekeepers apparently believe that environmental planning is boring to most people, and they may well be right.

These observations apply to environmental-planning efforts everywhere and are not unique to the Niagara Frontier. Those who believe that it is important for citizens' views to be represented accurately in environmental planning must find some means other than the traditional ones for incorporating those views into the process.

Niagara Frontier Study

Recognizing these citizen-participation difficulties, a research group in the Environmental Studies Center at the State University of New York at Buffalo sought a more efficacious means for improving representation in the development of the water-quality plan for the Niagara Frontier region. We reasoned that a well-designed and -executed survey study could improve representation in two important respects. First, by interviewing a random sample of a thousand people from the region, we could obtain the views on environmental matters of an accurate representation of all types of people to be found in the broad public. Second, a well-designed and lengthy interview (seventy minutes on the average) could obtain the beliefs and attitudes of these people on a wide variety of environmental matters and related concerns. Specific beliefs on water quality can be seen in perspective because they are embedded in an overall set of environmental and economic beliefs and attitudes. Seen in context, environmental beliefs are more representative then if elicited only as specific responses to a single question.

The Rockefeller, Ford, and Kettering foundations supported the proposed survey. An interview schedule was carefully designed in cooperation with the 208 planning staff and was thoroughly pretested. During the summer and early fall of 1976, interviews were obtained by the university's Survey Research Center with 1,021 persons sixteen years of age and older, selected randomly from the two-county region. In addition, a similar interview was administered to 233 leaders by the staff of the Environmental Studies Center. Leaders were sampled randomly from different sectors of leadership in the two counties. They were representative of those leaders who were most likely to participate in the development of the water-quality plan or in its implementation (Wirth, Sedransk, and Reitan 1977).

The information from this first wave of interviews was fed into the 208 planning process when the plan had been underway for about six months. The planning process continued for approximately one additional year with the proposed plan alternatives being presented to the public in the first three months of 1978. At the same time as many of the respondents from the broad public sample as could be reached (about 63 percent) were reinterviewed by telephone. Similarly mail questionnaires were sent to all of the leader respondents; about 77 percent responded. These follow-up interviews were designed to update our knowledge of public thinking on environmental matters and, in particular, to seek the preferences of the public and leaders for the various water-quality-plan alternatives and provide this information to the planning group.

Strengths and Weaknesses of Surveys

The survey study should not be viewed as a substitute for traditional modes of participation but rather as a supplement. A survey is static and is not an adequate substitute for the dynamic interaction and development of ideas that can occur in face-to-face discussion. Probably the survey is best seen as a corrective for distorted interpretations that may result from participation by a tiny fraction of the public, many of whom will be participating to serve special interests. A survey has the unique capability of incorporating the views of the uninterested but affected public who would have no other form of representation were it not for the survey.

A related purpose might be characterized as societal myth testing. In every society, every community, there are widely held beliefs that constitute a set of assumptions (a context) that underlie public discourse. These beliefs are perceived as so universally accepted that people take them as assumed; often they are not articulated. Some of these beliefs will be well based on reality, and others may, in fact, be a myth. A thorough, competent sample survey is the only methodology available for differentiating myth from reality.

Myth Testing

Some public myths were rather convincingly refuted by the data. For example, it is widely believed, not only on the Niagara Frontier but in the country as a whole, that most of the public believes that providing jobs must be traded off against environmental protection. Yet 80 percent of both the broad public and the leaders in the sample believed that we can have both enough jobs and a clean environment and that we need not choose between them. Furthermore 62 percent of the broad public believed that improving water quality would create rather than lose jobs, another 28 percent believed that it would have no effect, and only 10 percent thought that it would have the effect of losing jobs. This information was fed back to community leaders. Yet in the second-wave interviews the largest proportion of leaders believed *that the public would believe that water clean-up would lose jobs.*

We also asked this question: "Planning to do what is best for the community can interfere with our freedom to do what we want as individuals. Should we keep our freedom to do what we want or should we do what is planned as best for the community?" Seventy percent of the public chose planning over freedom; yet when the leaders were asked how the public would answer that question, more than half of them predicted that the public would select freedom over planning.

It is often supposed that most people believe that growth is good and that most people would wish their area to grow in population. The Niagara Frontier has in fact nearly stopped growing. When respondents were asked if they would be better off if the area grew in population or better off if it stayed about the same size, 80 percent preferred that it stay the same size. But approximately half of the leaders preferred the area to grow rather than stay the same size, and an even larger percentage predicted that the public would wish the area to grow in population.

It is widely assumed that most people would prefer to consume more and more consumer goods. To see what the public really believes we asked, "Many people seem to believe that consuming more things leads to a better quality of life; others say we can find quality of life without consuming more things. What do you think; should we as a nation continue to consume more or should we slow down on consumption?" Eighty percent of the public and the leaders believe that we should slow down on consumption, yet when the leaders were asked how the public would answer that question, 60 percent predicted that the public would prefer to continue to consume more.

The reinterviews with the public were especially designed to provide leaders with feedback from the public concerning their preference for plan alternatives. Even though the respondents were informed in the question that the more-ambitious clean-up plan would require higher taxes, they clearly indicated (60 to 22 percent) that they preferred the more-ambitious plan. Leaders were about evenly divided between the two plans but, when predicting public response, they guessed most frequently that the public would be opposed to both plans. When this information was shared with local leaders, they continued to advocate the less-ambitious plan. The public preference was communicated to state and federal environmental officials as well and very likely affected their review of the local planning effort.

Reception of Information Provided to Community Leaders

If the findings from a survey study are to be incorporated meaningfully into the development of an environmental plan, it is essential that the leaders who develop or implement the plan receive and accept those findings. Our second wave of interviews with the leaders gave us an opportunity to explore the extent to which the information from the survey was received and also how the leaders reacted to it. Every one of the leaders interviewed on the first wave had been sent a copy of the major findings from that wave (Milbrath 1977).

We are reasonably confident, through personal observation, that those involved with the day-to-day planning efforts (the planning staff and their committee of supervisors) did read the report. In fact, we appointed a member of our research team as a liaison to the Planning Board to help ensure maximum utilization of the survey findings.

The leadership sample included many persons who were not involved on a day-to-day basis with the planning effort. They tended to be people who represented important interest groups or who would be important for the implementation of the plan. Our second wave of interviews provided an opportunity to inquire if they recalled receiving the report that we mailed to them; 63 percent recalled receiving the report. Of those who recalled receiving it, 61 percent (42 percent of the total) reported reading it through and 23 percent (14 percent of the total) reported studying it carefully. Those who reported having read through the report were asked how they reacted to it on six different reaction dimensions arranged in a semantic differential format. (See table 11-1.) Most of these leaders found our report interesting, easy to understand, believable, useful, and somewhat surprising. Despite this favorable reaction to the report, however, it seems to have done very little to change their outlook.

The fact that only 14 percent of the leaders studied the report carefully is not surprising but still troubling. One can understand that leaders are busy and could not be expected to read every report with care. The low percentage reading with care, however, suggests that survey researchers

Table 11-1
Reactions of Leaders Who Read Survey Report

	33%	31%	29%	Neutral 6%	1%	0%	0%	
Interesting	33	31	29	6	1	0	0	Uninteresting
Not believable	0	3	4	8.5	18	37	30	Believable
Surprising	3	15.5	20	24	17	11	10	Not at all surprising
Not at all useful	1	1	3	13	31	33	17	Very useful
Easy to understand	17	33	24	17	3	4	1	Confusing
Changed my outlook	1	11	18	22.5	6	24	17	Didn't affect my outlook

who are generating information that should influence a planning effort will have to make special efforts to get their message through. A study that is well executed but unread is a study largely wasted.

The staff of the Environmental Studies Center made several public presentations of its findings to the community. Leaders were asked if they recalled observing such a presentation; 22 percent reported that they had. Those persons who had observed a presentation were asked how they reacted to it; the findings are reported in table 11-2. In contrast to those who had merely read the report, those who observed the presentations found it even more interesting, believable, and useful but not as surprising. They reported about equal ease in understanding the information, and the report was a bit more likely to have changed their outlook. Nearly all of these presentations generated very vigorous discussion, and there was plentiful opportunity for those in the audience to challenge and test the accuracy of the findings. This discussion seems to have removed some of their reactions of surprise and to have enabled the findings to make more impact.

Conclusions from Our Experience

Considerable effort was devoted to gathering information that would be useful to the 208 planners. Did they in fact find it useful? One of the consulting firms used information from the study to weight some of the factors in its computer model. Community coordinators were hired by the planning agency to stimulate public participation. The coordinators had found this to be a very difficult task, and our survey study added an extra dimension of representation that they welcomed because it helped to reassure the EPA monitors that the regional planning effort had a strong public-participation component.

Beyond that, our study was not given much attention by the local 208 planners. It was reported to us that some of the leaders were resentful that our data showed that many of the leaders held inaccurate perceptions of the public's views on many issues. Additionally many of the leaders preferred to relax environmental standards in order to stimulate economic growth and did not wish to accept our findings that people were willing to pay additional taxes in order to bring the area's waters up to a level of quality that was safe for swimming.

The survey findings did generate considerable interest at the state, regional, and national level of environmental agencies. Over fourteen hundred copies of our basic first report were distributed throughout the country (Milbrath 1977). Presentations were made to the State Department of Environmental Conservation in Albany, Region 11 of EPA in New York City, EPA officials in Washington, D.C., a national meeting of environmental information officers, and several other 208 planning regions.

Table 11-2
Reactions of Leaders Who Observed Presentation of the Findings

				Neutral				
	38.5%	20.5%	28%	8%	3%	3%	0%	
Interesting								Uninteresting
Not believable	0	0	5	18	16	24	37	Believable
Surprising	3	8	10.5	32	26	10.5	10.5	Not at all surprising
Not at all useful	0	3	0	10.5	34	29	24	Very useful
Easy to understand	16	40	21	13	8	3	0	Confusing
Changed my outlook	3	10.5	26	26	8	18	8	Didn't affect my outlook

There are some curious anomalies in the reactions to the survey information. Although the survey attracted considerable interest at the local, state, and national level, local leaders still found it difficult to accept our findings. Most of them reacted very positively to the survey information, yet they also reported that it did not affect their outlook. This anomaly is partially explained by a well-known psychological need. Most persons in a community who have risen to a leadership position pride themselves that they have arrived at their positions on public issues after careful research and analysis. They recognize that other people hold different positions but, in most cases, they are quite convinced that their personal position is correct. Given that situation, it is extremely unlikely that a survey study, no matter how well conducted or how surprising its findings, will have much effect on that outlook. The most that could be expected would be the opening of a wedge or the raising of a doubt. The findings of a survey study could have considerably more impact on those who are undecided or uncommitted, but such persons are not very likely to be found in leadership positions.

A related barrier is that most planners, civil servants, and political leaders are not trained in the interpretation and usage of survey data. Such work does not fit into any of their standard routines; therefore a rather imaginative planner or leader is required to recognize how it might be used to maximum advantage. Given that situation, the impact of the study is more likely to occur in subtle rather than forthright, obvious ways. The leader who has been hesitant, fearing that the public might be unwilling to accept a step that he or she would like to propose, may feel encouraged to go ahead. An argument over probable public reactions that might have occurred does not take place because the data suggest what the public tends to believe. One should not expect data of this sort to change minds or turn heads. This kind of study is more likely to reinforce and encourage certain actors and may stimulate those in opposition to firmer resolve.

A survey study of use of research by governmental decision makers showed that officials were inclined to reject information when the results were counterintuitive, that they were willing to accept findings uncritically if they were intuitively satisfying, that political implications of findings appear to override any other consideration in determining utilization, and that officials' feelings about the reliability of data, though an important factor in utilization, are less important than objectivity or political feasibility (Caplan, Morrison, and Stambaugh 1975, paraphrasing findings drawn from Kochen 1977).

Another difficulty that we experienced in gaining acceptance of our findings resulted from the 208 planning process itself. Many reports from around the country indicate that 208 planning has been chaotic and/or poorly supported. Apparently a few planning groups simply gave up before completing a plan. The two-year planning effort on the Niagara Frontier had four different directors, three of whom resigned before completing their task. Their resignations stemmed, at least in part, from their frustrations with the planning process. This lack of continuity in leadership greatly affected the way that our information was used in the planning process. A director who had worked with us at the project-planning stage to acquire certain information was no longer in that position to receive and utilize the information when it was available.

Many people have asked for further information on the methodology and findings of the survey, but to our knowledge, no other studies patterned after it have been launched. Of the approximately 250 plans of this sort developed around the country, apparently only three or four have used survey studies. Those other surveys were much simpler and had inadequate funding for conducting a well-designed study. The thoroughness and complexity designed into the Niagara Frontier study are intimidating to most planning agencies in that they would not have the expertise and would not have budgeted for the expense (approximately $100,000). This expense is not prohibitive, however; many guidelines recommend that 10 percent of a planning effort be devoted to citizen participation. If a planning contract was let for $2 million, as many are, $200,000 could be devoted to citizen participation, allowing $100,000 for a survey and another $100,000 for a healthy traditional citizen-participation effort. Because lack of expertise is probably a greater intimidating factor than the cost of the study itself, planners who recognize the value of a survey study as a supplement to a public-participation effort would be well advised to seek the assistance of experts at a local university to help plan and execute it.

At a more fundamental level, a basic difficulty is that many planners do not value public participation in their work. Being more accustomed to maps and statistics, many are uncomfortable dealing with people. A planner who does not place much value on citizen participation does not allocate sufficient resources in the budget to obtain useful information from the public. Many planners perceive that they must fulfill a planning contract in a limited period, and they tend to perceive public participation as diversionary from meeting that objective. From the side of the public, there is very little clamor to get involved in the planning process; thus planners can ignore the public without suffering serious consequences.

Given the current situation, there is great doubt that the public can meaningfully be brought into the environmental-planning process. Meaningful citizen involvement will not happen unless the planners themselves strongly value public participation and make special efforts to incorporate public views into the process. There are a myriad of ways that clever planners can ignore or deflect public input if it does not suit their purposes, particularly if the public itself does not feel a strong urge to insert its views into the plans. Utilizing a survey study to provide an extra dimension of representation in environmental planning can be successful, but only if the planning agency wants the data and participates actively with the survey staff in designing the study and in analyzing the results. Many other academic and public values can be realized from a study such as ours that make it worthwhile, but it is unlikely that the impact on the plan itself will be the major one.

References

Caplan, N.; Morrison, A.; and Stambaugh, R.J. 1975. *The Use of Social Science Knowledge in Policy Decision at the National Level.* Ann Arbor: Institute for Social Research, University of Michigan.

Kochen, Manfred. 1977. "Information Systems for Work Models." In Karl Deutsch et al., *Problems of World Modeling.* Cambridge, Mass.: Ballinger.

Milbrath, Lester W. 1977. "An Extra Dimension of Representation in Water Quality Planning: A Survey Study of Erie and Niagara Counties, New York, 1976." Occasional Paper 1. Buffalo: Environmental Studies Center, State University of New York.

Stewart, James M., ed. 1974. "Proceedings: Conference on Public Participation in Water Resources Planning and Management." Chapel Hill: Water Resources Research Institute, University of North Carolina.

"Symposium on Public Participation in Resource Decision Making." 1976. *Natural Resources Journal* 16 (January).

U.S. Environmental Protection Agency. 1976. "Public Participation Handbook for Water Quality Management." Washington, D.C.: Government Printing Office.

Wirth, George; Sedransk, Joseph; and Reitan, Paul. 1977. "Strategies for Selection of a Leadership Sample in Applied Survey Research: A Case Study in Erie and Niagara Counties, New York, 1976." Occasional Paper 5. Buffalo: Environmental Studies Center, State University of New York.

12 The Study of Political Feedback Using Nonrecursive Causal Models: The Case of State Divorce Policies

Gillian Dean

Scholars concerned with political accountability and governmental responsiveness need a better empirical understanding of political feedback, or the extent to which policies reflect and respond to the people they are intended to affect. Political scientists, policy analysts, and others have long acknowledged the need for research in the area of political feedback, but little has been done to satisfy this need (Easton 1965; Deutsch 1966; Fowler and Lineberry 1972). Like many other provocative questions in the political world, feedback does not lend itself easily to rigorous analysis. An interest in political feedback prompts a careful look at those aspects of the policy process that happen after governmental policies are formulated and before they are modified. But these aspects of the process are difficult to conceptualize, measure, and assess empirically (Dean 1975).

Ideally quantitative research on policy feedback would rely on time-series data and models that reflect temporal lags between policy impacts and subsequent policy decisions. When these data are not available, nonrecursive causal models can be used to elaborate correlation relations between policies and their consequences because they allow researchers to inquire about policy impacts and political feedback at the same time. One question is how people are really affected by the policies aimed at them. Another question is how people's responses influence changes in these policies, or how responsive policies are to the impacts they engender. These general research concerns can be diagrammed in this way:

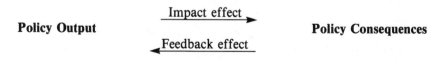

Policy Output ⟶ Impact effect ⟶ **Policy Consequences**
⟵ Feedback effect ⟵

The research reported here employs a nonrecursive approach to feedback and impact in a study of state divorce policies. States enjoy broad powers to regulate many areas of public morality and the family, and the

113

past fifteen years have seen dramatic changes in state divorce policies. In most states, divorces are easier to obtain than they were in the past. In the same period, there have been marked increases in state divorce rates. The study focuses upon the interrelations between divorce policies and divorce behavior or rates. The major questions concern impact—do more-permissive divorce policies lead to higher divorce rates?—and feedback—do differences in divorce rates affect differences in divorce policies?

Model and Control Variables

Impact and feedback are assessed in the context of other influences on state divorce rates and policies. Earlier studies of divorce behavior stressed three contextual factors other than laws that influence divorce rates. In areas where education, income, and social stability are higher, divorce rates are lower (see Udry 1966; Cutright 1971; Fenelon 1971; Plateris 1961; Kephart 1966; Goode 1962). These variables are included in the causal model as exogenous variables that influence divorce rates.

There has been virtually no research on the feedback effects of divorce, but general discussions of feedback processes suggest six variables in addition to divorce rates that may influence the responsiveness of divorce policies to divorce behavior in a state:

1. Public opinion that favors permissive divorce policies will encourage permissive policies.
2. State political culture is the particular area pattern of orientation to political and policy action. According to this concept developed by Elazar (1966), states with more-traditional values are expected to have less-permissive divorce policies (see also Patterson 1968).
3. Church interest groups and area religious culture can influence policies significantly. The model posits that states with large Catholic populations will have more-restrictive divorce policies (see Fairbanks 1979; Elliott 1950).
4. Legislative professionalism can influence divorce policies (Grumm 1971). The more professional the state legislature, the more likely it is to keep up with citizen demands, and the more permissive its divorce policies will be.
5. Legislative apportionment can influence divorce policies. Well-apportioned legislatures, in which urban and other groups are more equitably represented, are more likely to create permissive laws (see Grumm 1968; Pulsipher and Weatherby 1969).
6. Innovative states are expected to be more responsive to divorce rates and hence more likely to adopt and implement permissive divorce policies than are states that are not innovative in their policies (Walker 1969).

Measuring the Variables

The permissiveness of state divorce policies is measured as the policies are implemented in the judicial system rather than as they are enunciated in legal statutes. This avoids the ambiguity of statutes, which have different meanings in different states, and simplifies the model by eliminating additional factors that can intervene in the translation of laws into practice (see Rheinstein 1972; Stetson and Wright 1975).

Four aspects of divorce policy are used to measure permissiveness: cost of divorce, amount of time it takes to get a divorce, how carefully jurists hear divorce cases, and ease of obtaining a divorce in a state compared with other states. Data for these measures were obtained from a questionnaire mailed nationwide to 519 professors and lawyers concerned with family law (Dean 1975). These data were combined in an additive, standardized index.

Divorce rates are measured by the number of final decrees granted in 1970 per 1,000 married women between the ages of fourteen and fifty. This measure provides the rate of divorce in relation to the population most likely to divorce; older married women, who are less exposed to the risk of divorce, are excluded. Data are not readily available concerning migratory divorces (those obtained in a state where neither party is a bona-fide resident), but estimates suggest that migratory divorce constitutes only about 3 or 4 percent of the divorce in the United States (Cahan 1932; Jacobsen 1959; Plateris 1971), and in this study's questionnaire, experts on divorce estimated migratory divorce at 2.9 percent of the national total. However, such divorces make up 25 to 30 percent of the total divorces in Nevada, and Nevada is therefore excluded from the analysis.

Data for divorce rates are from 1970, but data for some of the other variables are not available for this time period. For example, the policy questionnaire records information for 1973, and some of the measures for the second set of control variables were taken before 1970. However, in most instances it would have been inappropriate to measure these variables as of 1970 because their effects on divorce policy and divorce rates work over a longer period.

The three variables that affect the impact of divorce policies on divorce rates are measured using U.S. Census data (Dean 1975):

1. Income: Per-capita personal income for 1970.
2. Education: 1970 median education level of women in the state. (Women are considered because the base for the divorce rate is derived from the number of women in the state.)
3. Social stability: Intercounty migration rates for 1970.

Intercorrelations among these three control variables are weak, except in the case of income and education, where the correlation is reasonably high

($r = .57$). This suggests that the regression results must be interpreted with care to avoid problems with colllinearity.

The variables affecting the linkage between divorce rates and policies are measured as follows (Dean 1975):

1. Mass public opinion: A 1959 Gallup survey, modified by Weber (1971) to indicate state-level public preferences on divorce policies.
2. Political culture: Sharkansky's (1969) translation of Elazar's (1966) observations of state cultures. The index increases in value as states are more traditionalistic.
3. Religion: The percentage of the state's population that is Catholic, used because there are no data directly reflecting the strength of religious culture or Catholic interest groups in the states.
4. Legislative professionalism: The Grumm (1968) index, which taps legislative pay, session length, staffing, and other services.
5. Apportionment: The David-Eisenberg (1961) index of urban under-representation.
6. Innovativeness: Walker's (1969) index of state policy adoption.

Several of these control variables are highly intercorrelated (see table 12-1). Because this collinearity would make it difficult to interpret regression results, factor analysis is used to reduce the number of variables while retaining most of the information they contain. A principal-components analysis of the six variables shows the presence of two underlying factors. (See table 12-2; the rotation is orthogonal.) First, the environment factor reflects the social environment of the feedback process. Political culture, public opinion, and percentage Catholic weigh heaviest on this factor. Public opinion has a negative loading on the factor; the other two major variables have positive loadings. These signs show that states with proportionally higher populations of Catholics are in fact states with more-permissive divorce policies, supported by public opinion and political culture. Second, the institutions factor reflects the way in which political in-

Table 12-1
Intercorrelations of Control Variables

	Opin	Cult	Cath	Prof	Innv	Malp
Public opinion						
Political culture	− .501					
Percent Catholic	.441	− .403				
Professionalism	.192	.005	.260			
Innovation	.518	− .459	.502	.652		
Malapportionment	.325	− .403	.502	.300	.602	

Table 12-2
Principal Components Analysis

	Environment Factor	Institutions Factor
Political culture	.865	.166
Public opinion	−.749	.071
Percent Catholic	.662	.342
Professionalism	−.034	.946
Innovativeness	.540	.749
Malapportionment	.580	.471

stitutions determine divorce policies. On this factor, the high loading variables are innovativeness, professionalism, and apportionment. States with high scores on either the environment or the institutions factors are expected to have more-permissive divorce policies.

Analysis of the Model

The first hypothesized linkage is that where divorce policies are more restrictive, divorce rates are lower. Education, income, and social stability are also expected to affect divorce rates. The second major hypothesis is that divorce rates will have a feedback effect on divorce policies. The institutions and environment factors are also expected to influence policies. Using the following notation:

DIV	= divorce rate	MIG	= migration rates (social stability)
POL	= divorce policy	ENV	= environment factor
EDUC	= education level	INST	= institutions factor
INC	= income level		

these two sets of linkages can be combined and their reciprocal relationships expressed as a set of interdependent simultaneous equations:

$$POL = a + b_{11}DIV + b_{12}EDUC + b_{13}INC + b_{14}MIG + e_1 \quad (12.1)$$

$$DIV = a + b_{21}POL + b_{22}INST + b_{23}ENV + e_2. \quad (12.2)$$

Ordinary least squares is an inappropriate estimation procedure in this situation, so a simple and applicable alternative procedure, two-stage least squares, is used to evaluate the model (Theil 1971, chaps. 9-10). The structural form of the model is shown in equations 12.3 and 12.4, with the estimated coefficients as given by the two-stage procedure. The numbers under the coefficients are Student's t values. These values are significant at the .10 level when $t \geq 2.01$; they are significant at the .05 level when $t \geq 2.68$.

$$DIV = 9.88 + 6.181 \text{ POL} - .744 \text{ EDUC} + .022 \text{ INC} + .350 \text{ MIG}$$
$$\quad\quad (.728)\ (2.059)\quad\quad (.508)\quad\quad\quad (.797)\quad\quad (1.391)$$

$$(12.3)$$

$$POL = -.992 + .072 \text{ DIV} - .190 \text{ INST} - .144 \text{ ENV}$$
$$\quad\quad (2.254)\quad\quad (2.579)\quad\quad (2.026)\quad\quad (1.810).$$

$$(12.4)$$

Estimated results show that divorce policy strongly affects divorce behavior and that divorce behavior has an important effect on policy.

In equation 12.3, which predicts divorce rates, divorce policy is positively related to rates. The estimated coefficient for policy is substantively large and statistically significant, suggesting that more-permissive policies lead to higher divorce rates. Policy is the only statistically significant determinant of divorce rates. Migration is statistically almost significant, but neither education nor income is. The collinearity between income and education may be distorting the significance tests for the estimates of these two variables. However, when either income or education is omitted from the basic model, the remaining of the two variables is still an insignificant determinant of divorce. The basic conclusion is that divorce appears to be more responsive to policy than to the other, less manipulable, factors.

Equation 12.4, which predicts divorce policies, indicates that as divorce rates increase, divorce policies become increasingly permissive. The environment factor's negative relation to divorce policy suggests the policy strength of Catholic groups. Even in states whose political culture and public opinion support permissive divorce policies, larger proportions of Catholics result in more-restrictive policies. Divorce policies appear to be more responsive to religious interests than to public opinion or area culture.

The institutions factor shows a surprising result. States with more-innovative, better-apportioned, and more-professional legislatures are more likely to have more-restrictive policies in the context of the model. This may be explained partly by the very restrictive divorce policies and strong state legislatures of several northeastern and New England states; by contrast, the southern states, often endowed with less-energetic state governments, tend to have more-permissive policies. Another possible explanation is that innovativeness and professionalism are directed more toward policies affecting group interaction and benefits and less toward concern with individual relationships. Further research on the effects of region and on the nature of professionalism and innovation may explain this finding better.

Because the two major variables, divorce policy and divorce, are measured in very differently scaled metrics, we also consider the standardized regression coefficients. For the equation in which divorce rate is the dependent variable, the standardized regression coefficient for divorce policy is 0.729. This is not much higher than the standardized coefficient for divorce rates (0.610) where the policy is the dependent variable. This suggests that the scaling differences mask the fact that the impact link from policy to divorce is about as strong as the feedback link from divorce to policy.

The coefficients of determination for the structural equations, while not small, suggest that a sizable proportion of the variance remains unexplained by the model. Analysis of the residuals, however, showed no far outliers and no clearly discernible patterns.

Summary and Implications

This analysis indicates that restrictive divorce policies tend to decrease the incidence of divorce, while higher divorce rates lead to more-permissive divorce policies, at least as these are practiced in the courts. One can infer from these findings that the more-permissive divorce laws to which almost all states are turning will in fact promote divorce. The findings also suggest that states will tend to respond to demands for divorce by liberalizing their divorce policies.

The study relies on cross-sectional rather than time-series data, and its reciprocal modeling does not precisely and comprehensively reflect dynamic impact and feedback processes. Evidence about cross-sectional differences can be suggestive of the form and nature of change over time; however it cannot let us say whether the demand for divorce will create a spiral of more-liberal policies, followed by increased demands, followed by more-liberal policies. If we view increases in divorce as a siphoning off of pent-up demand for divorce, which could not be satisfied under more-onerous legal procedures, a divorce threshold is plausible. This would mean that no matter how easy obtaining a divorce became, the demand for it would not exceed this threshold level.

This research also points to the utility of nonrecursive causal models for the analysis of other types of political feedback. Recent policy changes beckon researchers to examine reciprocal feedback relations in the development and modification of no-fault legislation. No-fault laws, which allow couples to dissolve marriages with no discussion of who is to blame, have impacts that are far-ranging and often unanticipated; their feedback consequences are as yet uncharted.

One set of unexpected effects has shown up in the implementation of no-fault laws. The new legal approach has obscured many of the old guidelines that courts used to have for dividing the money in marriage. No-fault usually means that property is reassigned to both spouses rather than routinely handed over to one. Under this system, issues of property valuation and accounting figure importantly, and lawyers and judges find contested cases increasingly difficult and time-consuming ("Disputes over Money" 1980). Many divorce courts are experiencing long and growing delays. Where no-fault requirements tax the resources of people charged with carrying out the law, feedback effects are hard to predict. They may include changes in the no-fault requirements, changes in the implementation process (such as separate family courts or special divorce examiners), or some form of mutual adaptation where both the law and its implementation are altered.

Other feedback effects of no-fault can be traced through the way in which policies affect the attitudes of citizens. Divorce court is about the most common introduction that Americans get to their judicial system. But delay and complexity in the divorce process do not give many clients a good impression of the courts. Future research may inquire about citizen reactions and their consequences. To the extent that no-fault prompts negative reactions to the divorce system, do these reactions color general attitudes toward the legal system? Have these reactions led more couples to consider marriage or remarriage more carefully or to protect themselves with antenuptial agreements? Are judges and legislators aware of the effects that divorce policies have on behavior and attitudes? Under what conditions do they adjust policies and practices to counter unfavorable consequences?

The nonrecursive modeling approach suggested here allows detailed models of the divorce process to capture and assess such possibilities. In the same way, intriguing questions about feedback in other areas of policy change can be examined. This approach encourages researchers to develop theory that includes reciprocal relations, and it makes possible the empirical analysis of feedback effects that political research has not yet widely explored.

References

Cahan, A. 1932. *Statistical Analysis of American Divorce*. New York: Columbia University Press.

Cutright, P. 1971. "Income and Family Events: Marital Instability." *Journal of Marriage and the Family* 33:291-306.

David, Paul T., and Eisenberg, Ralph. 1961. *Devaluation of the Urban and Suburban Vote*. Charlottesville: University of Virginia.

Dean, G. 1975. "Impact and Feedback Effects: Divorce Policies and Divorce in the American States." Ph.D. dissertation, University of Wisconsin.

Deutsch, K. 1966. *The Nerves of Government: Models of Political Communication and Control*. New York: Free Press.

"Disputes over Money and Children Swamp U.S. Divorce Courts." 1980. *Wall Street Journal*, 28 January.

Easton, D. 1965. *A Systems Analysis of Political Life*. New York: John Wiley.

Elazar, D.J. 1966. *American Federalism: A View from the States*. New York: Thomas Y. Crowell.

Elliot, M.A. 1950. "Divorce Legislation and Family Stability." *Annals of the American Academy of Political and Social Sciences* 252:134-147.

Fairbanks, D. 1979. "Politics, Economics and the Public Morality." *Policy Studies Journal* 7:714-721.

Fenelon, B. 1971. "State Variations in the United States Divorce Rate." *Journal of Marriage and the Family* 33:321-327.

Fowler, E.P., and Lineberry, R.L. 1972. "Patterns of Feedback in City Politics." In D.R. Morgan and S.A. Kirkpatrick, eds., *Urban Political Analysis: A Systems Approach*, pp. 361-367. New York: Free Press.

Goode, W.J. 1962. "Marital Satisfaction and Instability: A Cross-Cultural Class Analysis of Divorce Rates." *International Social Science Journal* 14:507.

Grumm, J. 1968. "Structural Determinants of Legislative Output." Paper presented to the Conference on the Measurement of Politics in the American States, Inter-University Consortium for Political Research, Ann Arbor, Michigan.

_____ . 1971. "The Effects of Legislative Structure on Legislative Performance." In R. Hofferbert and I. Sharkansky, eds., *State and Urban Politics*. Boston: Little, Brown.

Jacobsen, P. 1959. *American Marriage and Divorce*. New York: Rinehart.

Kephart, W.M. 1966. *The Family, Society and the Individual*. 2d ed. Boston: Houghton Mifflin.

Patterson, S.C. 1968. "The Political Culture of the American States." Journal of Politics 30:187-209.

Plateris, A. 1961. "Marriage Disruption and Divorce Law in the United States." Ph.D. dissertation, University of Chicago.

_____ . 1971. "The Statistics of Divorce." In B.N. Adams and T. Weirath, eds., *Readings on the Sociology of the Family*. Chicago: Markham.

Pulsipher, A.G., and Weatherby, J.L., Jr., 1968. "Malapportionment, Party Competition and the Functional Distribution of Governmental Expenditures." *American Political Science Review* 62:1207-1219.

Rheinstein, M. 1972. *Marriage Stability, Divorce and the Law*. Chicago: University of Chicago Press.

Sharkansky, I. 1969. "The Utility of Elazar's Political Culture." *Polity* 2:66-83.

Stetson, D.M., and Wright, G.C. 1975. "The Effects of Laws on Divorce in American States." *Journal of Marriage and the Family* 37:537.

Theil, H. 1971. *Principles of Econometrics*. New York: John Wiley.

Udry, J.R. 1966. "Marital Instability by Race, Sex, Education and Occupation, Using 1960 Data." *American Journal of Sociology* 72:203-209.

Walker, J.L. 1969. "The Diffusion of Innovation among the American States." *American Political Science Review* 63:880-899.

Weber, R.E. 1971. *Public Policy Preferences in the States*. Bloomington: Institute of Public Administration, University of Indiana.

13 Termination Policy and the Menominees: Feedback of Unanticipated Impacts

Nicholas C. Peroff

In the 1950s Congress adopted a national policy to promote rapid termination of the federally protected tribal status of American Indians. Among other things, the new policy was designed to abolish Indian reservations and terminate any special recognition accorded to Indian tribes because of their distinct identity as legally independent Indian nations. The ultimate goal of termination policy was the accelerated assimilation of all native Americans into the larger American society.

The overall impact of termination on native Americans was enormous. Vine Deloria, a noted native American author, refers to the termination era in Indian policy as "the most traumatic period in Indian existence" (Deloria 1978, p. 87). By the time the last tribe was terminated in 1962, 13,263 tribal members had been "freed" by Congress and over 1,365,800 acres of tribal lands had been removed from the protection of federal trust status (Butler 1978, p. 52).

Prior to congressional enactment and President Eisenhower's signing of the Menominee Termination Act in 1954, the Menominees were considered one of the most self-sufficient Indian tribes in the United States. They owned a 220,000-acre forest in Wisconsin and operated a sawmill representing a capital investment of $1.5 million. Moreover, the tribe had accumulated $10 million on deposit in the U.S. Treasury. Viewed as one of the most "advanced" tribes in the nation, the goal of the Menominee Termination Act was to move the Menominees toward full assimilation as rapidly as possible.

Unanticipated Impacts of Termination

In this study, the unanticipated impacts of Menominee termination generally refer to the consequences of termination that made rapid assimilation less likely or even impossible. In 1961, after several years of delay, caused in part by tribal reluctance to plan and prepare for termination, the Menominee Reservation became Wisconsin's seventy-second county. The implementation of termination was complete. Several unanticipated im-

The research for this chapter was supported, in part, by a faculty research grant from the University of Missouri-Kansas City.

pacts emerged before final implementation of the policy. Expenses involved in the preparation for termination, along with other factors, nearly exhausted the tribe's cash assets. After a lack of funds forced the closure of the tribal hospital, tuberculosis became a major health problem. Menominee children born after the date of closure of the tribal rolls in 1954 were no longer legally members of their own tribe. Badly needed sources of leadership were depleted when economic decline and rising anxieties about the future led many of the younger and more-educated Menominees to move away from the tribe.

Policy impacts occurring after the implementation of Menominee termination evolved throughout the 1960s and into the early 1970s. The termination act accelerated the rate of assimilation among a minority of the tribe's membership; however, the unanticipated impacts of the policy frustrated a realization of the primary goal of Menominee termination. While varying in importance, a number of unanticipated impacts can be attributed, at least in part, to the implementation of the Menominee Termination Act.

Economic Instability

Prior to termination, living conditions on the Menominee Reservation were certainly not affluent, but the tribe had nearly achieved economic self-sufficiency. After termination the small population of thirty-four hundred residents and an economy tied almost exclusively to an unstable market for raw forest products could not provide sufficient local tax revenues to run new county governmental operations and services. Even after years of continuous direct and indirect federal and state aid, the county could not raise revenues necessary for matching federal grants-in-aid. Tribal leaders were compelled to take the extremely unpopular move of selling former tribal land to non-Menominees as recreational home sites in order to prevent a fiscal collapse of the county.

Unemployment

Before termination the Menominee mill ran under a community-service philosophy. Work was organized to create employment, and anyone willing to work was hired. After termination the mill stressed operational efficiency and a more traditional business philosophy for its employment practices. With the adoption of modernized milling techniques, the overall number of jobs available was reduced. Menominee unemployment reached annual rates of 18 to 28 percent, and seasonal rates approached 40 percent.

Although milling operations were significantly expanded, fewer jobs were available in 1970 than in 1961.

Elimination of Public Services

Bureau of Indian Affairs (BIA)-administered health, education, and utility services were ended with termination. Free dental care, the reservation hospital, and a resident doctor were no longer available to Menominee families after 1961. Despite major grants of federal and state transitional aid, the new county barely provided minimum services for its residents. By 1970 over 40 percent of the Menominees had applied for welfare and other supplemental aids and services.

Loss of Tax-exempt Status

While on their reservation, Menominees did not pay a personal property tax. After termination they were taxed near the maximum rate allowed by state statutes. Tax evasion was a serious problem, and many individual Menominees were threatened with prosecution for unpaid taxes.

Aggravated Racial Discrimination

In 1972 the BIA asserted that "termination has resulted in a generation of Menominees with little better than a ninth-grade education and an almost 75% dropout rate" (U.S. Department of the Interior 1972, p. 9). There are insufficient data to support the BIA's conclusion that poor Menominee educational achievement was caused by termination since the average grade level attained actually increased slightly after termination. However, evidence suggests that the incidence of discrimination against Menominee school children increased with the merger of Menominee schools with a nearby non-Indian school district. A 1972 report by the regional civil rights director of the U.S. Office of Civil Rights concluded that less adequate and effective educational services were provided for Menominees than for white children after the merger (Mines 1972).

Political Alienation

Like most other Americans, Menominees have never been completely satisfied with every aspect of government in the United States. However, the experience of termination clearly increased tribal dissatisfaction with the political system. Nearly all tribal references to federal, state, and local government were expressed in negative terms. It became common to think that all of the Menominees' problems were "the result of a plot by malicious Government officials" (U.S. Senate 1965-1966, pp. 31-35).

Renewed Factionalism

Tribal factionalism has always been present in Menominee society. However, after termination, division within the tribe assumed a level of intensity rarely experienced on the reservation. Widespread Menominee frustrations with tribal life after termination were displaced upon tribal leaders. The development and sale of county land as recreational home sites for non-Menominees was attacked as a misconceived strategy designed to make a bad policy work. Many Menominees also feared the loss of political control of their county as non-Menominees began establishing permanent residences within the former reservation.

Opposition to Tribal Leadership

For several years, opposition to termination was confined to sporadic verbal attacks on the policies of tribal leaders. In 1970 that opposition began to coalesce, forming a new political organization, DRUMS (Determination of Rights and Unity for Menominee Shareholders). The growth of organized Menominee resistance to assimilation provided by DRUMS was the most salient unanticipated impact of termination.

Reaction of DRUMS to Termination

DRUMS was first organized outside Menominee County among Menominees living in Milwaukee and Chicago. After several months, a chapter of DRUMS was formed within the county. The urban origin of the organization paralleled national patterns of rising Indian activism in the United States in the 1960s. Many new groups advocating "red power," such as the American Indian Movement (AIM), began to organize in several major metropolitan areas. Confronted with life in the cities, urban Indians became more sensitive to their status as a racial minority and many of them, particularly the young and more educated, organized to fight for their rights as native Americans. Many nonresident Menominees were particularly angry over the sale of Menominee County land to non-Menominees. They considered tribal ownership of their ancestral land as the strongest surviving basis for their common Indian identity.

Repeal of the termination act became DRUMS's primary goal, but it was not the immediate objective of the organization. DRUMS leaders concluded that the political climate in Wisconsin and in Congress was not receptive to a campaign to reverse termination. They decided instead to pursue a set of indirect strategies designed to overthrow the established tribal leaders and gain a controlling influence over Menominee affairs. First, they mobilized a loyal group of supporters both within and outside the county. Second, they focused their demands by making direct personalized attacks on tribal leaders and their policies. Third, DRUMS organized public demonstrations to disrupt the sale of county land to non-Menominees. Fourth, they solicited favorable media coverage for their organization and objectives. Fifth, DRUMS initiated a series of court actions designed to harass and delay the development and sale of county land. Finally, DRUMS representatives initiated a lobbying effort in the Wisconsin state capital and in Congress to gain support for their objectives from state and federal public officials.

After termination, control of the sale of land to non-Menominees and, more generally, management of the entire economy of the county was placed in the hands of a tribally owned corporation, Menominee Enterprises Inc. (MEI). Taken together, DRUMS's strategies had a devastating effect on the corporation and recreational land sales. Litigation costs severely cut into corporate profits, land sales were depressed due to buyer anxiety over dissension within the tribe, and potential outside investment in new business ventures within the county remained out of reach because of the prevailing political instability.

Despite the success of DRUMS's tactics, the traditional Menominee leaders remained in control of county government and the corporation, so in 1971 DRUMS adopted a new tack. DRUMS candidates ran for positions on the MEI board of trustees as vacancies became available. The new strategy was a spectacular success. By the end of 1972, DRUMS held seven of eleven positions on the board. Its campaign for county offices was less successful. However, because of MEI's controlling influence over county affairs, DRUMS, in effect, had overthrown and replaced the traditional tribal leadership when it took over management of the corporation.

DRUMS's campaign to gain control of the course of tribal affairs indirectly instilled in the tribe a new sense of political awareness and pride in their identity as native Americans. The new organization renewed Menominee interest in tribal politics. Eventually voter turnout in Menominee County rose from a low of 2 percent in 1969 to 49 percent in 1973 (U.S. House 1973, p. 40). DRUMS also revived Menominee interest in the affairs and future of the entire tribe by acting as a liaison between

Indians living in and outside the county. With their renewed sense of individual pride and self-confidence, the tribe stood ready to pursue a repeal
of the Menominee Termination Act and the restoration of their former
reservation.

National Rejection of Termination Policy

As America moved through the 1960s, the federal government abandoned
its termination policy. One reason was a growing national sensitivity to the
rights and special problems of all minorities, including native Americans.
America's perception of itself was changing. The long-held view that
American society should be a melting pot where various ethnic and culturally
distinct groups eventually meld into a homogeneous whole was challenged
by a new concept, cultural pluralism. When the concept reflects reality,
culturally distinct groups within the society such as native Americans are accepted as legitimate subdivisions of the society. They may retain their
distinctiveness but are still accorded the same rights and public privileges,
the same access to political and economic advantages, and the same responsibilities as all other members of the total society (Yinger and Simpson
1978).

The widespread emergence of intensified native American political activism was a second reason for federal abandonment of Indian termination.
The increase in native American militancy brought greater national attention to the needs and demands of American Indians and increased pressures
on all levels and branches of government to respond to native American
grievances.

Finally the unanticipated impacts of termination policy on all native
Americans also brought about a demand for a change in national Indian
policies. Despite the fact that "money was literally being poured into Indian
country" from such programs as the Office of Economic Opportunity's
Community Action Project for Indian Reservations, the BIA's Division of
Economic Development, and the Department of Health, Education and
Welfare's Office of Indian Progress, American Indians were afraid to take
full advantage of the opportunities offered (Butler 1978, p. 56). If, as a
result of the programs, they became more self-sufficient, they feared they
would again become targets of an aggressively pursued policy of termination.

To ease these fears and encourage greater tribal participation in his anti-
poverty programs, President Johnson in 1968 delivered a speech to Congress, "The Forgotten American." In it he called for an end to termination
and the beginning of a new "policy of maximum choice for the American
Indian, a policy expressed in programs of self-help, self-development,

self-determination" (Johnson 1968). President Nixon reaffirmed the words of his predecessor in 1970 when he recommended that Congress adopt a new policy to provide for Indian self-determination "without termination of the special federal relationship with recognized Indian Tribes" (Nixon 1970). While the words of presidents and other federal officials were appreciated, American Indians remained skeptical. As long as the Menominees remained a terminated tribe, they still felt that termination represented a latent, but real, threat to their tribal way of life.

The abandonment of further Indian termination had little direct impact on the Menominees. They were already a terminated tribe. Congress would not act on its own initiative to restore the Menominees's tribal status and reservation. The issue was insignificant when compared to other business that demanded congressional attention. If restoration was to become a reality, the tribe would have to seize the initiative and press Congress for repeal of the Menominee Termination Act.

Menominee Restoration

After DRUMS unified the tribe around the objective of restoration, DRUMS leaders adopted a general strategy that could be termed the politics of conscience. Noting the tactics of the civil-rights campaign, migrant workers, and other social-protest movements of the 1960s, DRUMS recognized the importance of the American conscience in American politics. DRUMS leaders projected the tribe as a subjected minority who desired only the restoration of their rights as native Americans. The strategy won the support of numerous individuals and groups across the nation who felt morally bound to help the tribe combat injustices caused by the policy of termination.

The political sophistication of the tribe's new generation of leaders is also reflected in many of the specific strategies employed in the drive for restoration. Within the tribe, DRUMS initiated a petition to Congress calling for restoration, sponsored a letter-writing campaign to all members of the Wisconsin congressional delegation, and organized a 220-mile "March for Justice" from Menominee County to Wisconsin's state capital Madison. Outside the tribe, DRUMS leaders launched an extensive lobbying and public-information campaign directed toward Wisconsin public officials, other Indian tribes across the nation, key members of Congress, the BIA, members of the Nixon administration, and numerous private organizations throughout the nation.

On 22 December 1973, the Menominee tribe achieved its objective. Congress's acknowledgment that the policy of Indian termination had been a mistake, a growing national awareness and sensitivity to minority rights, and the Menominees's forceful opposition to termination culminated in the enactment of the Menominee Restoration Act. The act restored federal recognition and protection to the Menominee tribe and reestablished nearly all of its former reservation. The act also provided concrete evidence to all native Americans that the era of Indian termination was over.

The Menominees are still recovering from the disastrous effects of termination. Although continued federal economic and community-development funds are needed, projects such as a recent major renovation of the tribe's sawmill and the construction of a new health clinic demonstrate that the tribe is moving in a very promising direction. Their new tribal government embodies the essence of native American demands for maximum Indian participation in the planning and administration of federal policies and programs for native Americans.

Summary and Conclusion

The rapid acceleration of native American assimilation into the larger American society was the major goal of Indian termination policy. Congress initiated its ill-fated assimilation strategy by passing the Menominee Termination Act of 1954. In socioeconomic and psychological terms, the unanticipated impacts of the act on the welfare of the tribe were disastrous. Individual tribal dissatisfaction with termination eventually coalesced to become the most significant unanticipated impact of Menominee termination. Armed with renewed determination and a greater capacity to resist involuntary assimilation, DRUMS frustrated the attainment of the policy objectives of the Menominee Termination Act. Contrary to the goals of termination, the Menominee people today are at the forefront of a new era in Indian affairs that has brought native Americans greater self-determination over their own tribal affairs and future than at any other time in recent American history.

National Indian policy currently is in a state of dangerous uncertainty. Rising anti-Indian sentiment and increasingly unsympathetic congressional reaction to several controversial court decisions on Indian land and water claims in Maine, Washington, and elsewhere may prompt the federal government again to disregard the treaty-guaranteed rights of native Americans and search for a new solution to what some consider the "Indian problem." The Menominee experience suggests that a return by Congress to policies dedicated to the forced assimilation of Indians would be indefensible. Future policies must not deny native Americans their legal, treaty-defined rights to the cultural and political autonomy they desire.

References

Butler, Raymond V. 1978. "The Bureau of Indian Affairs: Activities since 1945." *Annals of the American Academy of Political and Social Science* 436 (March):50-60.

Deloria, Vine, Jr. 1978. "Legislation and Litigation Concerning American Indians." *Annals of the American Academy of Political and Social Science* 436 (March):86-96.

Johnson, Lyndon B. 1968. "The Forgotten American." Presidential message to Congress, 6 March.

Mines, Kenneth A. 1972. Correspondence from the Regional Civil Rights Director, U.S. Office of Civil Rights, to Arnold Gruber, Superintendent, Shawano Board of Education, 4 October.

Nixon, Richard M. 1970. "Message from the President of the United States Transmitting Recommendations for Indian Policy." House of Representatives, Document 91-363, 8 July.

U.S. Department of the Interior. Bureau of Indian Affairs. 1972. "The General Economic Situation of the Menominee Indian Tribe of Wisconsin." Report to the House Committee on Appropriations and Interior and Insular Affairs Committee, 31 March.

U.S. House of Representatives. 1973. "Hearings before the Subcommittee on Indian Affairs of the Committee on Interior and Insular Affairs on H.R. 7411." 25-26 May, 28 June.

U.S. Senate. 1965-1966. "Hearings before the Subcommittee on Employment and Manpower of the Committee on Labor and Public Welfare on S. 1934." 10-11 November, 17 February.

Yinger, Milton, and Simpson, George. 1978. "The Integration of Americans of Indian Descent." *Annals of the American Academy of Political and Social Science* 436 (March):137-151.

Part IV
Research Methods

Focusing explicitly on methodological questions, the three chapters in this part, despite disparate focuses, illustrate varying needs in the analysis of policy impact. The need for specific methodological techniques is examined in the chapter by Kathryn Newcomer and Richard Hardy. Using as their subject matter the effect of reapportionment on state expenditures for large cities, they examine and identify the relative advantages and disadvantages of three different linear-trend models. The need for a substantive focus around which analytical methodology can be developed is presented in Marcia Ory's discussion of concepts and methodologies used in family-impact analysis. This type of analysis is important because it makes the analyst shift attention from a specific policy to an institution on which one or more policies have an impact. Ory carefully takes the reader through the steps necessary to perform family-impact analysis. A. Lori Manasse demonstrates the need for building into ongoing programs procedures for policy-impact analysis. Her study of a rehabilitation program for expelled students in the Los Angeles School District details how a comprehensive impact-analysis program can be established and operated as the particular policy is developed and implemented.

14 Quasi-Experimental Time-Series Designs in Policy-Impact Analysis

Kathryn E. Newcomer and
Richard J. Hardy

In recent years, policy analysts, as well as politicians, have shown great interest in assessing both short-term and long-term consequences of public policies. It is well recognized that knowledge of the time dimension underlying policy results constitutes a critical constraint on analyses of policy impact.

With this understanding, recent time-trend studies have attempted to depict the time dimension of policy consequences through extensions of regression techniques (McCrone and Hardy 1978; Lewis-Beck 1979; Albritton 1979; Hardy and Newcomer 1980). Trend models have been used to detect shifts in governmental expenditures, case loads, and enforcement actions that correspond to distinct changes (interruptions) in statutes or administrative policies. These models can help depict seasonal variations, as well as short- and long-term shifts in such governmental activities. Although such techniques are widely accepted, there appears to be little agreement as to which specific time-trend model is most appropriate for this endeavor.

At least three linear-trend models are prominent in the current policy literature. These models portray an interrupted time-series design, following the conceptual guidance of Campbell and Stanley's pioneering work (1963). Detailed discussions of each model can be found in Draper and Smith (1966) and Johnston (1972). While the models differ only slightly in form, the application of each could render significantly different interpretations concerning the impact of particular public policies. All three models correspond to a discontinuity research design and depict long-term shifts in governmental actions. Two of the models also depict clearly the short-term shift, and one model compares the postintervention trend to an expected slope value. Given various research objectives, which time-trend model is most useful in depicting policy impact? Are these models of equal utility in assessing both short-term and long-term policy consequences? And what are the relative advantages and disadvantages of each model?

One way to answer these questions is to compare the application of each model to the same time-series data. For this purpose we have monitored the change in per-capita state expenditures for large cities over a twenty-year period (1957-1977).[1] Recognizing the impact of both budgetary incrementalism and economic inflation upon expenditure patterns over time, the dependent variable is corrected by the consumer price index and logged to depict the linear trend in state spending for cities. Using each model in a quasi-experimental design, we sought to determine the impact of court-ordered reapportionment on these policy expenditures within eight states.

A Policy Problem: The Impact of Reapportionment

Since the Supreme Court held in 1964 that representation in both houses of state legislatures must be based on population (*Reynolds* v. *Sims*), there has been a great deal of speculation regarding the probable impact of reapportionment in the American states. While few question that court-ordered reapportionment has altered the composition of state legislative personnel, it is still uncertain whether reapportionment has had any significant impact on public policies. Scholars generally can be divided into two groups: "reformers" and "skeptics" (Bicker 1971).

Reformers believe that reapportionment will produce dramatic changes in the allocation of resources to urban areas as a result of the influx of predominantly liberal, Democratic legislators. Dines (1966) and Bryan (1967), for example, optimistically predict that reapportionment will cause significant shifts in policies relating to education, transportation, welfare, health, and aid to large cities. Subsequent empirical analyses lend partial credence to this view by suggesting that reapportionment has had a salutary effect on the distribution of benefits to urban areas (Pulsipher and Weathersby 1968; Hanson and Crew 1973).

Skeptics, on the other hand, such as Dye (1965), Hofferbert (1966), and Bicker (1971), contend that implementation of reapportionment in the states at best will have only nominal effects on public policies beneficial to urban concerns. As a case in point, Dye argues that "there is no empirical evidence that reapportionment will bring about any substantial changes in state programs in education, welfare, highways, taxation or in the regulation of public morality" (1966, p. 294). Support for this argument is found in analyses by Jacob (1964), Hofferbert (1966), and Brady and Edmonds (1967), who assert that policy outcomes are more products of a state's economic resources than whether a state is well apportioned.

Most of the research of both reformers and skeptics, however, has been based on either case studies or cross-sectional analysis, which do not allow researchers to measure the impact process systematically (Grumm 1977). For that reason, we turned to a quasi-experimental time-series analysis. A quasi-experiment is one in which the condition or state of an object can be measured before and after a treatment but where full experimental control of the treatment by the researcher is lacking (Campbell and Stanley 1963, p. 34). Time-series simply refers to the periodic evaluation of a variable following the introduction of an experimental change in order to detect discontinuity (*ibid.*, p. 55). For that reason, we selected both an experimental group and a control group of states.

Our experimental states (Maryland, California, Florida, and Kansas) were among the most malapportioned states before 1964 based on three indexes: the Dauer-Kelsay (1965) index of representativeness, the David-Eisenberg (1961) index of vote value, and the Schubert-Press (1964) apportionment score. By 1968 each of these states was relatively well apportioned. In contrast, our control states (Oregon, Massachusetts, Wisconsin, and Nebraska) were all well apportioned considerably before 1964.

We posit that if similar expenditure patterns are exhibited in both the experimental and control groups, then one could suspect that something other than reapportionment is responsible for the policy shift. Conversely should the experimental group register changes in policy that are significantly different from those of the control group, then it might be possible to suggest that reapportionment does have a policy impact. The three linear-trend models will be applied to our data to compare the spending trends before and after reapportionment. And estimates from the three linear-trend models applied to the data will be compared to discern the degrees of autocorrelation and multicollinearity and the relative reliability of the regression coefficients associated with the use of each model.

Three Linear-Trend Models

Model 1

We begin with a simple linear-trend model, employed by Hanson and Crew (1973) and Feig (1978):

$$\text{Log}_e(Y_{t1}) = a_1 + b_1 X_{1t} + u_{t1} \qquad (14.1)$$

$$\text{Log }(Y_{t2}) = b_2 + b_3 X_{3t} + u_{t2} \qquad (14.2)$$

where:

Y_{t1} represents per-capita policy expenditure, by state, before reapportionment, for $t = 1957$ through 1967 (the natural log of Y_{t1} is regressed).

Y_{t2} represents per-capita policy expenditure, by state, after reapportionment, for $t = 1968$ through 1977 (the natural log of Y_{t2} is regressed).

X_{1t} represents a time trend before reapportionment, 1957 through 1967, where $X = 1$ for 1957, 2 for 1958, . . . , and 11 for 1967.

X_{3t} represents a time trend after reapportionment, 1968 through 1977, where $X = 1$ for 1968, 2 for 1969, . . . , and 10 for 1977.

u_{t1} represents the error term before reapportionment.

u_{t2} represents the error term after reapportionment.

In this model, a_1 estimates the *level* of policy expenditure at the beginning of the time series (1957); b_1 estimates the *slope* of policy expenditure before reapportionment; b_2 estimates the *level* of policy expenditure in 1968; and b_3 estimates the *slope* of policy expenditure after reapportionment. The immediate advantage of this model is its simplicity (see figure 14-1). A major drawback, however, is that in order to determine the difference in slopes b_3 and b_1, and therefore to determine the long-term policy impact, one must calculate separate t-tests.[2] Since separate regressions are made on the two time series (preintervention and postintervention), one must have a fair number of time points in the "after" period.

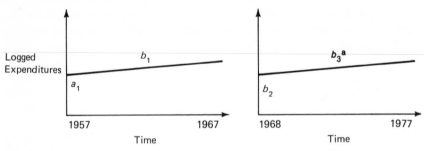

[a]We use b_2 and b_3X_{3t} rather than a_2 and b_2X_{2t} to afford a direct comparison with the other linear-trend models.

Figure 14-1. Diagram of Model 1

Model 2

This multiple-regression model is exemplified in the works of Masters (1975) and McCrone and Hardy (1978):

$$\text{Log}_e(Y_t) = a_1 + b_1X_{1t} + b_2X_{2t} + b_3X_{3t} + u_t \qquad (14.3)$$

where:

Y_t represents per-capita policy expenditures, by state, for $t = 1957$ through 1977 (the natural log of Y_t is regressed).

X_{1t} represents a time trend before reapportionment from 1957 through 1967, and a constant thereafter, where $X = 1$ for 1957, 2 for 1958, . . . , 11 for 1967, and 11 for 1968 through 1977.

X_{2t} represents a division in prereapportionment and postreapportionment periods, 0 before and 1 after ($X = 0$ for 1957 through 1967 and 1 for 1968 through 1977).

X_{3t} represents a time trend after reapportionment, a constant from 1957 through 1967, and a time trend after ($X = 0$ for 1957 through 1967, and 1 for 1968, 2 for 1969, . . . , 10 for 1977).

u_t represents the error term.

In model 2, a_1 estimates the level of policy expenditure in 1957; b_1 estimates the slope of policy expenditures before reapportionment; b_2 estimates the increment in policy expenditure between 1967 and 1968; and b_3 estimates the slope of policy expenditure after reapportionment. Model 2 is more parsimonious than model 1 is, and it allows the researcher to see at a glance the relative magnitude and direction of the two slopes b_1 and b_3 (see figure 14-2). Moreover, the coefficient of the dummy variable, b_2, allows one to see the difference in the levels of expenditure before and after reapportionment. However, as in model 1, in order to find significant long-term impact, it is necessary to conduct separate t-tests for differences in slopes $b_3 - b_1$.

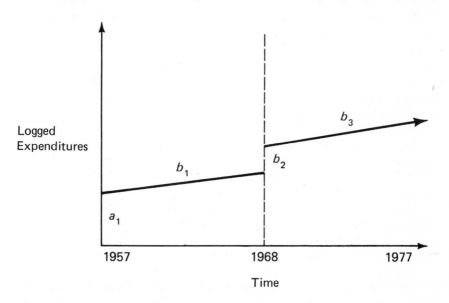

Figure 14-2. Diagram of Model 2

Model 3

The final time-trend model is suggested by Cook and Campbell (1976) and Lewis-Beck (1979):

$$\text{Log}_e(Y_t) = a_1 + b_1 X_{1t} + b_2 X_{2t} + b_3 X_{3t} + u_t \tag{14.4}$$

where:

Y_t represents per-capita policy expenditure, by state, for $t = 1957$ through 1977 (the natural log of Y_t is regressed).

X_{1t} represents a time trend from 1957 through 1977, where $X = 1$ for 1957, 2 for 1958, . . . , 21 for 1977.

X_{2t} represents a division in prereapportionment and postreapportionment periods, 0 before and 1 after, where $X = 0$ for 1957, 0 for 1958, . . . , 1 for 1968, 1 for 1969, . . . , 1 for 1977.

X_{3t} represents a time trend after reapportionment, 0 before, a counter after, $X = 0$ for 1957, 0 for 1958, . . . , 0 for 1967, 1 for 1968, 2 for 1969, . . . , 10 for 1977.

u_t represents the error term.

In model 3 parameter a_1 estimates the level of policy expenditure in 1957; b_1 estimates the slope of policy expenditures across the entire time series; b_2 estimates the increment in level of policy expenditure from 1967 to 1968; and b_3 estimates the increment in slope of policy expenditure after reapportionment, above the slope across the entire period. The advantage of this model is that both significant long-term and short-term policy patterns can be detected readily by merely examining the coefficients b_2 and b_3 (see figure 14-3). However, in this mode X_{3t} is an interactive term and thus is extremely correlated with X_{1t} and X_{2t}.

Based on the information in tables 14-1, 14-2, and 14-3, it appears that reapportionment has had neither short-term nor long-term effects in this policy area since significant changes were recorded for both the experimental and control states with all three models.

As expected, there are some differences in the estimates derived from the three models. Our criteria for assessing the relative utility of each model include degrees of multicollinearity, degrees of autocorrelation, and the reliability of the regression coefficient estimates (see table 14-4).

Multicollinearity, which has only somewhat recently received adequate attention (Farrar and Glauber 1967; Gordon 1968), refers to the degree to which independent variables are intercorrelated when using ordinary least

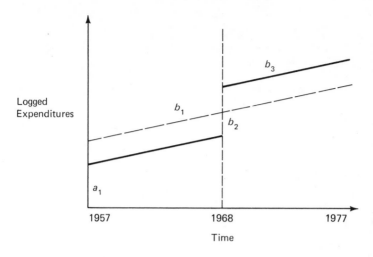

Figure 14-3. Diagram of Model 3

squares (OLS) estimation techniques. As the level of multicollinearity goes up, decreasing the likelihood that individual parameters will show statistical significance, the estimates are rendered less reliable.

There is no multicollinearity with the first model because it includes only one trend variable. The simple correlations among the independent variables for the other models appear in table 14-5. As is evident, models 2 and 3 exhibit high correlations among the three trend variables, averaging .75 in model 2 and .85 in model 3. The level of multicollinearity is higher in the third model than in the second, but the correlations among the trend variables are all quite high, signaling that caution must be used in interpreting the estimates. Fortunately, none of the simple correlations between the independent variables exceeds the total multiple R for the equations, which, according to Farrar and Glauber (1967), indicates that the distortion of estimates may not be too damaging. Also the majority of the estimates in both models are statistically significant when the total F for the equations are significant.

To deal with the multicollinearity in models 2 and 3, one could transform the variables into first-order differences or go to an ARIMA model (Albritton 1979). A combination of the trend variables would be difficult to justify theoretically. The main point to keep in mind is that if the models are used only for predictive purposes, the multicollinearity will not be a problem. In using quasi-experimental time-series designs to assess policy impact, the relative explanatory effects of individual independent variables are not of interest anyway.

Table 14-1
Estimated Long- and Short-term Impact of Reapportionment on State Expenditures for Large Cities Using Model 1

State	a_1	b_1	b_2	b_3	$(t_{b_3-b_1})$	$DW_1{}^a$	$DW_2{}^a$
Control							
Oregon	1.85 (.069)	.07[b] (.010)	3.07[b] (.152)	.00 (.027)	−2.41[b]	.8	2.2
Wisconsin	3.47[b] (.063)	.07[b] (.009)	4.15[b] (.062)	.03[b] (.011)	−2.86[c]	1.3	1.5
Nebraska	1.00[b] (.138)	.07[b] (.020)	2.26[b] (.247)	.11[b] (.044)	.83	1.7	.7
Massachusetts	3.94[b] (.096)	.10[b] (.014)	4.39[b] (.161)	.08[b] (.029)	−.63	.9	2.2
Experimental							
Maryland	4.09[b] (.045)	.11[b] (.007)	5.53[b] (.077)	.06 (.014)	−3.13[c]	1.2	.9
California	2.62[b] (.069)	.08[b] (.010)	3.70[b] (.059)	.01 (.010)	−5.00[c]	1.1	1.1
Florida	−2.45[b] (.923)	.18 (.136)	−.24 (.412)	.51[b] (.073)	2.14[b]	1.9	1.1
Kansas	1.57[b] (.059)	.02[b] (.009)	2.81 (.331)	.04 (.059)	.34	1.0	.7

Notes: Large cities are defined as those with populations of 200,000 or more.

Figures in parentheses under coefficient estimates are standard errors of those estimates.

[a] DW_1 and DW_2 represent Durbin-Watson statistics (d) for equations 14.1 and 14.2.

[b] Coefficient is statistically significant at 0.05 level.

[c] Coefficient is statistically significant at 0.01 level.

Table 14-2
Estimated Long- and Short-term Impact of Reapportionment on State Expenditures for Large Cities Using Model 2

State	a_1	b_1	b_2	b_3	$\overline{R}^2$	F	DW
Apportioned							
Oregon	1.85[a] (.103)	.07[a] (.015)	.38[a] (.155)	.00 (.021)	90	48.3[b]	2.2
Wisconsin	3.47[a] (.060)	.07[a] (.009)	-.15 (.089)	.03[a] (.012)	92	60.7[b]	1.4
Nebraska	1.00[a] (.178)	.07[a] (.026)	.46 (.268)	.11[a] (.036)	90	49.3[b]	1.4
Massachusetts	3.94[a] (.119)	.10[a] (.018)	-.77[a] (.179)	.08[a] (.024)	77	17.6[b]	1.8
Malapportioned							
Maryland	4.09[a] (.057)	.11[a] (.008)	.13 (.085)	.06[a] (.011)	98	310.6[b]	1.7
California	2.62[a] (.062)	.08[a] (.009)	.12 (.094)	.01 (.012)	95	102.4[b]	1.3
Florida	-2.45[a] (.733)	.18 (.108)	.06 (1.103)	.51[a] (.146)	81	22.3[b]	1.8
Kansas	1.57[a] (.200)	.02 (.030)	.99[a] (.301)	.04 (.040)	85	31.0[b]	1.1

Notes: Large cities are defined as those with populations of 200,000 or more.

Figures in parentheses under coefficient estimates are standard errors of those estimates.

[a]Coefficient is statistically significant at 0.05 level.

[b]Coefficient is statistically significant at 0.01 level.

Table 14-3
Estimated Long- and Short-term Impact of Reapportionment on State Expenditures for Large Cities Using Model 3

State	a_1	b_1	b_2	b_3	R^2	F	DW
Control							
Oregon	1.85[a] (.103)	.07[a] (.014)	.45[a] (.147)	-.07[a] (.026)	.90	48.3[b]	2.2
Wisconsin	3.47[a] (.059)	.07[a] (.009)	-.08 (.085)	-.03[a] (.014)	.92	57.4[b]	1.4
Nebraska	1.00[a] (.178)	.07[a] (.026)	.52[a] (.254)	.05 (.044)	.90	49.3[b]	1.4
Massachusetts	3.94[a] (.123)	.10[a] (.018)	-.68[a] (.169)	-.02 (.030)	.77	17.6[b]	1.8
Experimental							
Maryland	4.09[a] (.057)	.11[a] (.088)	.24[a] (.081)	-.05[a] (.014)	.98	310.6[b]	1.9
California	2.62[a] (.053)	.08[a] (.077)	.20[a] (.089)	-.07[a] (.018)	.96	102.4[b]	1.2
Florida	-2.45[a] (.741)	.18 (.109)	.24 (1.143)	.33 (.182)	.81	22.3[b]	1.8
Kansas	1.57[a] (.200)	.02 (.030)	1.01[a] (.285)	.02 (.050)	.85	31.0[b]	1.1

Notes: Large cities are defined as those with populations of 200,000 or more.
Figures in parentheses under coefficient estimates are standard errors of those estimates.
[a]Coefficient is statistically significant at 0.05 level.
[b]Coefficient is statistically significant at 0.01 level.

Table 14-4
Comparison of Linear-Trend Models: Multicollinearity, Autocorrelation, and Reliability of Coefficients

Criterion	Model 1	Model 2	Model 3
Multicollinearity	No problem	Problem	Problem
Percentage of Durbin-Watson (d) statistics, which are > 1.0 and < 3.0	68.8%	100.0%	100.0%
Percentage of X_{1t} coefficients that are significant at .05 level	87.5	75.0	75.0
Percentage of slope differences that are significant at .05 level ($b_{3t} - b_{1t}$ in models 1 and 2)	62.5	50.0	50.0
Percentage of X_{3t} coefficients that are significant at .05 level	62.5	62.5	50.0

Autocorrelation, or the presence of serially correlated error terms, presents a problem endemic to the application of OLS techniques to time-series data. Serially correlated disturbances lead to deflated estimates of the sampling errors of the coefficient estimates so that t and F values, as well as multiple Rs, are inflated. Thus the coefficients and variance explained are more likely to be statistically significant, leading to incorrect rejection of null hypotheses. The Durbin-Watson statistic (d) is the most common test for autocorrelation. If the value of d is roughly close to 2, then the null hypothesis for no autocorrelation is accepted (Kelejian and Oates 1974, pp. 200-207). Autocorrelation appears problematic only in the first of our linear-trend models. Almost one-third of the equations applying model 1 showed d statistics that deviated from the acceptance range (1.0 to 3.0), so the bias toward unjustified rejection of the null hypothesis in the first model should be kept in mind.

Higher levels of multicollinearity tend to reduce the likelihood of statistically significant coefficient estimates, while autocorrelation exaggerates their statistical significance. Thus both problems affect the reliability of the estimates. As would then be expected, there are more statistically significant coefficients with the first model than with the other two, which also reflects the extent of autocorrelation in the first and multicollinearity in the other two models.

In an interrupted time-series design, differences between trends (slopes) in policies before and after a policy intervention are of central concern, so

Table 14-5
Simple Correlations among Independent Variables in Models 2 and 3

	X_2	X_3
Model 2		
X_1	.79	.65
X_2		.82
Model 3		
X_1	.86	.88
X_2		.82

one may be less concerned with overexaggeration or underexaggeration of statistical significance than is true with other regression analyses. However, it is most desirable to use the most conservative method of assessing policy impact with this design (that is, the most restrictive procedure for rejecting the null hypothesis). As table 14-5 illustrates, models 2 and 3 are more conservative than the first model in discerning significant differences between the slopes of interest. Given model 2's lack of autocorrelation, and lower level of multicollinearity than model 3, it appears to be the most reliable estimator for our purposes.

Conclusion

This study demonstrated the use of three linear-trend models in depicting policy impact in a quasi-experimental time-series design. The rationale behind such a quasi-experimental design was elaborated in its application here to the question of the impact of the Supreme Court's reapportionment decisions upon patterns in state expenditures for cities. All three linear-trend models failed to show a discernible impact of the Court's decisions as both short-term and long-term gains for the cities were registered in both experimental and control states. However, there were differences of note in the findings associated with the three models.

The levels of multicollinearity and autocorrelation in the linear-trend models applied to the reapportionment example varied, depending upon the number and nature of the trend variables included in the models. Noting the impact of multicollinearity and autocorrelation upon the reliability of the coefficient estimates, we urge caution in the use of the models. For the purposes of this quasi-experimental design and any other similar tests of trends in expenditures before and after policy innovations, the most conservative estimate of differences in postinnovation trends is recommended. Expected seasonal shifts or responses to other socioeconomic factors should also be incorporated in a model.

This analysis highlights only obvious criteria that should guide decisions on the use of the linear-trend models in assessing policy impact. The use of more-sophisticated models (such as, ARIMA models) deserves more discussion, as does the application of linear-trend models to more-complex policy impact problems. Clearly more effort is merited to provide a better match of substantive questions of policy impact with appropriate linear-trend models, and it is hoped that this discussion will initiate more dialogue along these lines.

Notes

1. Data sources include "Finances of Individual Cities and Selected Urban Towns and Townships of over 50,000," in annual editions of *City Government Finances* (Washington, D.C.: Government Printing Office), and U.S. Department of Commerce, Bureau of the Census, U.S. Statistical Abstract, *Purchasing Power of the Dollar: 1940 to 1977* (Washington, D.C.: Government Printing Office, 1977).

2. The formula used to compute t-statistics for these time series is as follows:

$$t = \frac{b_3 - b_1}{3^2 + 1^{-2}}.$$

References

Albritton, Robert B. 1979. "Measuring Public Policy: Impacts of the Supplemental Security Income Program." *American Journal of Political Science* 23 (August):558-578.

Bicker, W. 1971. "The Effects of Malapportionment in the States—A Mistrial." In Nelson Polsby, ed., *Reapportionment in the 1970s*, pp. 151-200. Berkeley: University of California Press.

Brady, David, and Edmonds, Douglas. 1967. "One Man, One Vote—So What?" *Transaction* 4 (March):41-46.

Bryan, Frank M. 1967. "Who Is Legislating?" *National Civic Review* 56 (December):627-633.

Campbell, Donald T., and Stanley, Julian C. 1963. *Experimental and Quasi-Experimental Designs for Research*. Chicago: Rand McNally.

Cook, Thomas D., and Campbell, Donald T. 1976. "The Design and Conduct of Quasi-Experiments and True Experiments in Field Settings." In Marvin D. Dunnette, ed., *Handbook of Industrial and Organizational Psychology*. Chicago: Rand McNally.

Dauer, Manning J., and Kelsay, Robert G. 1965. "Unrepresentative States." In Glendon Schubert, ed. *Reapportionment*. New York: Charles Scribner's Sons.

David, Paul T., and Eisenberg, Ralph. 1961. *Devaluation of the Urban and Suburban Vote*. Charlottesville: University of Virginia.

Dines, Allen. 1966. "A Reapportioned State." *National Civic Review* 55 (February):74-78.

Draper, N.R., and Smith, H. 1966. *Applied Regression Analysis*. New York: Wiley.

Dye, Thomas R. 1965. "Malapportionment and Public Policy in the States." *Journal of Politics* 27 (August):586-601.

Farrar, Donald E., and Glauber, Robert R. 1967. "Multicollinearity in Regression Analysis: The Problem Revisited." *Review of Economics and Statistics* 49:92-107.

Feig, Douglas G. 1978. "Expenditures in the American States: The Impact of Court-ordered Legislative Reapportionment." *American Politics Quarterly* 6 (July):309-324.

Gordon, Robert A. 1968. "Issues in Multiple Regression." *American Journal of Sociology* 73:592-616.

Grumm, John G. 1977. "The Consequences of Structural Change for the Performance of State Legislatures: A Quasi-Experiment." In Susan Welch and John G. Peters, eds., *Legislative Reform and Public Policy*, pp. 201-213. New York: Praeger Publishers.

Hanson, Roger A., and Crew, Robert E. 1973. "The Policy Impact of Reapportionment." *Law and Society Review* 8 (February):69-93.

Hardy, Richard J., and Newcomer, Kathryn E. 1980. "The Impact of Reapportionment on Policy Expenditure: A Quasi-Experimental Time-Series Analysis, 1957-1977." *Law and Policy Quarterly* (forthcoming).

Hofferbert, Richard I. 1966. "The Relation between Public Policy and Some Structural and Environmental Variables in the American States." *American Political Science Review* 60 (March):73-82.

Jacob, Herbert. 1964. "The Consequences of Malapportionment: A Note of Caution." *Social Forces* (Winter):246-261.

Johnston, Jay. 1972. *Econometric Methods*. New York: McGraw-Hill.

Kelejian, Harry H., and Oates, Wallace E. 1974. *Introduction to Econometrics: Principles and Applications*. New York: Harper and Row.

Lewis-Beck, Michael S. 1979. "Maintaining Economic Competition: The Causes and Consequences of Antitrust." *Journal of Politics* 41 (February):169-191.

McCrone, Donald J., and Hardy, Richard J. 1978. "Civil Rights Policies and the Achievement of Racial Economic Equality, 1948-1975." *American Journal of Political Science* 22 (February):1-17.

Masters, Stanley H. 1975. *Black-White Income Differentials: Empirical Studies and Policy Implications*. New York: Academic Press.

Pulsipher, Allan G., and Weathersby, James L. 1968. "Malapportionment, Party Competition, and the Functional Distribution of Governmental Expenditures." *American Political Science Review* 62 (December):1207-1219.

Reynolds v. *Sims*. 1964. 377 U.S. 533.

Schubert, Glendon, and Press, Charles. 1964. "Measuring Malapportionment." *American Political Science Review* 58 (June):302-327.

15 Family-Impact Analysis: Concepts and Methodologies

Marcia G. Ory

The impetus for a systematic analysis of the impact of public policies and programs on family life has come from a variety of public and private sources. Most notable are the 1972 U.S. Subcommittee Hearings on Children and Youth (U.S. Congress 1974); an initial document, "Developing a Family Impact Statement," commissioned by the Foundation for Child Development (Kammerman 1976); the Family Impact Seminar, a program at the Institute for Educational Leadership at the George Washington University, designed to bring together leading scholars and policy makers on the family; and federal sponsorship of graduate-level training programs in family-impact analysis, one of which was at the Minnesota Family Study Center, University of Minnesota.

Development of Family-Impact Analysis

Although there is a growing rediscovery of the importance of the family, to date there has been no comprehensive, explicit policy for American families. Rather what is becoming increasingly evident is that family policy in the United States is characterized by an array of piecemeal, fragmented, and often inconsistent policies that affect the family in both intended and unintended ways. Concerned with the rapidly changing structure of the American family and the relationship of the family to other social institutions, policy makers, administrators, and the general public alike are beginning to recognize the importance of learning how public and private policies affect American families.

Family-impact analysis (FIA) is being developed as a tool for systematically examining and thus anticipating how alternative policies, programs, and services affect different aspects of family life. The product of FIA is a family-impact statement, which describes the current or projected effect of specified policies or programs upon all or particular types of families.

The research on which this chapter is based was supported by NIMH Training Grant 5 T32 MH 14619, "A Program for Training Family Impact Analysts." For a more complete description of the family-impact analysis model presented here, see Ory and Leik (1978). I am grateful to Reuben Hill and Robert Leik for their help in developing this research.

FIA can be thought of as a special case of the more general social-impact-assessment methodology. Family-impact assessment is not to be employed to the exclusion of other social and environmental assessments; instead familial impacts should be considered in conjunction with analyses at other levels. Unlike traditional social-science research, which often focuses on the relationship between background sociocultural factors and current attitudes and behaviors, FIA concerns alternatives that can be manipulated through policies and programs. Strategies may be borrowed from social-policy analysis, evaluation research, and forecasting and prediction techniques, but FIA is unique because of its emphasis on examining outcomes in terms of impacts on the family rather than on individuals or society as a whole. FIA is not a static process but a dynamic, iterative one; family-impact research is intended to affect policy making that may affect future family conditions, which, in turn calls for further policy making and research.

Characterization of Policy and Family Variables

A major concern of FIA is the specification of policy components that have potential impact on family life. Policies can be differentiated in terms of their stage of implementation—that is, whether the major focus is on the legal, regulatory, fiscal, or service-delivery aspects of the policy (Family Impact Seminar 1978). Policies and/or programs can be characterized further by whether they operate at a local, state, or national level; refer to public or private actions; and explicitly or implicitly are directed toward families. Although it can be argued that all activities potentially affect families in some way, health, education, welfare, economics, employment, and housing policies are thought to have the most direct impact on major aspects of family life.

In assessing familial impacts, it is important to determine how many, which type, to what extent, and in what way families are affected. All or some subcategories of families may be affected by the policy or program being examined. Impacts to be studied may be characterized as direct or indirect; intended or unintended; or short or long term. Both impacts that primarily affect structural characteristics of the family and those that primarily affect functional relationships within the family can be examined. Although family structure and functioning are obviously interrelated, family structure can be characterized by such factors as family size and type; stage in family life cycle; and family environments (that is, sociodemographic characteristics such as racial, ethnic, or class backgrounds).

Family functioning, on the other hand, refers to the performance of basic family tasks such as the ability to provide for the economic support and well-being of family members (the provider function); the provision of child-rearing and other nurturant, care-giving behaviors (the socialization-nurturant function); the initiation, maintenance, and dissolution of the family unit (the family-membership function); and the coordination and manipulation of informal and institutional resources for the benefit of family members (the resource-manipulation function) (Family Impact Seminar 1978). Family functioning also can be described by the nature and quality of interpersonal relationships among family members.

Strategies for Family-Impact Analysis

FIA can vary in methodological complexity. Some analyses call for an examination of existing laws and regulations; others require the generation of new data or the use of information already collected for other purposes. The complexity of analysis can range from the study of the impact of a specific policy on a particular family variable to the investigation of complex interrelationships between multiple policy and program factors and family impacts. Techniques for presenting the findings also vary from simple frequency distributions and graphs to two-variable cross-classifications to multivariate statistical techniques for testing and modeling complex interactions among variables.

General Framework for Family-Impact Analysis

The step-by-step procedure presented here represents a meshing of existing frameworks drawn from evaluation research methodology (Guttentag and Struening 1975; Rossi and Wright 1977; Suchman 1967), social-impact-assessment literature (Ukeles 1977; Vlachos et al. 1975; Wolf 1976), and earlier attempts at defining the process of family-impact assessment (Family Impact Seminar 1978; Mattessich 1977; McDonald 1978; Wilson and McDonald 1977).

Step 1: Identify Policy or Program for Analysis

It is likely that FIA will be initiated because a policy maker, administrator, or practitioner needs to know the familial impact of an existing or proposed policy or program. Although it is certainly important to understand the sociopolitical factors that influence the adoption of policies and programs, the family-impact analyst starts by asking how a certain policy(s) already affects or will probably affect families.

Step 1 entails two main substeps: selecting a policy or program for FIA and specifying relevant components of that policy or program.

Four factors should be considered in deciding whether to select a particular policy or program for FIA: whether the policy will have a probable impact on a sufficient number of families; the number of families who will be affected; how direct the family impact will be; and whether the policy has goals explicitly related to the family. In order to examine the relationship between the selected policy or program and family variables, it is necessary to review the policy's goals, regulations, and actual implementation components in order to specify what particular aspects of the policy will be considered in the analysis. Policies can be categorized by their major area of focus, domain, current status, and stage of implementation.

Step 2: Identify Family Impacts to be Examined

Just as it is important to identify specific policy components for analysis, it is necessary to specify expected family outcomes in terms of family structure and/or functioning for target populations. Both intended and unintended consequences should be examined. This step is composed of two related processes: the identification of target populations who will be affected by the policy and the specification of the ways in which target families will be affected.

Target populations can be identified in terms of their physical and sociocultural characteristics, as well as by key family variables such as family type and life-cycle stage. After one identifies target populations, it is important to specify what family characteristics are to be examined for possible impacts. One can ask if, and how, a selected policy or program will affect family-composition variables such as marital status or parental preferences; sociocultural factors such as the family's employment and financial status; or family-functioning tasks such as the family's ability to take care of and nurture its members. Other family outcomes of interest include how the policy affects the nature and quality of the internal family functioning. That is, does the policy change family decision making and division of labor among its members or affect the level of family cohesion?

Step 3: Specify the Relationship between the Policy or Program and the Hypothesized Family Impacts

Steps 1 and 2 presented a framework for categorizing policy components and family variables of interest. Now it is desirable to specify the connections between the policy and the predicted family outcome.

Step 3 has three substeps: defining the basic relationship between the policy and family factors; specifying the intervening factors linking the policy inputs to family outcomes; and considering external factors that might affect the basic relationships.

The first substep requires hypothesizing whether there is a direct relationship between the specified policy factors and predicted family impacts. Hypotheses about the relationship can come from several sources: one's own personal or professional experience, an informal poll of informed professionals from relevant disciplines, or systematic review of the literature. The second substep, specifying the intervening factors, requires examining the causal sequences that link the policy to the family outcome. Although the policy may be intended to affect the health and economic well-being of individuals, the second factor may affect family-membership patterns and activity levels (that is, who lives with whom and provides what care), which, in turn, have a secondary effect on the nature and the quality of family functioning. In the third substep, it is important to be aware of the social, economic, and political environment in which the policy and family factors are interacting. In order to distinguish real policy effects from spurious ones, the analyst needs to try to identify and control for effects of relevant external factors, such as the general state of the economy, the ideological climate, and/or technological innovations, which might be falsely exaggerating or masking the hypothesized relationship between policy components and family outcomes.

Step 4: Design and Implement Family-Impact Research

Having specified the relationship between specific policy components and family outcomes, the analyst should now design and implement a research strategy for determining whether the policy actually affects the family in the predicted way. The selection of the research design and analysis should be based on the primary purpose of the study; the availability of personnel time and financial resources for research; knowledge of advanced statistical techniques; and access to family-level data. There are two basic parts in step 4: identification of possible kinds of research strategies and information needed to determine familial impacts and implementation of the selected research strategy.

The first part of this step requires developing indicators of and planning strategies for obtaining information on all policy, familial, intervening, and external variables specified in the model. Indicators for most of the structural variables, such as socioeconomic status, family size, and life cycle, are relatively straightforward and often available in existing records and studies (Mattesich 1979). However, for the more qualitative indicators of family functioning, the analyst will need to designate how the different familial impacts are to be measured before planning other aspects of the research design.

In addition to identifying indicators for all major variables, the family-impact analyst needs to decide about the types and sources of possible information and how to sample those sources. When data are unavailable, or there are no resources for collection and analysis, the analyst might adopt any qualitative methodology, such as a review of existing literature, reliance on judgment by experts, or an examination of policy components and regulations to assess the probable family impacts. However, when they are accessible, quantitative data-based studies are advantageous because they allow for the collection of standardized information that can be analyzed in multiple ways, depending on the purpose and resources of the researcher.

Quantitative data-based studies are of two basic types: secondary analyses utilizing previously collected data and primary analyses in which information is obtained firsthand by interview, questionnaire, or direct observation. In a primary analysis, the researcher will need to determine the appropriate research design—experimental with a planned intervention(s) versus nonexperimental with no intervention to test—and sampling strategy (such as random, stratified, or purposive) and then design or borrow existing instruments for standardized data measurement.

Once the research strategy has been chosen, the second substep is to implement the selected design. Generally the research study probably will cost more and take longer to finish than originally expected. To facilitate implementation of primary data-based research in field settings, it is important to have planning and training sessions to foster open communication between the service and research staff so that each knows and respects the needs of the other.

Step 5: Assess Family Impacts of Each
Policy or Program Component

A variety of techniques for analyzing existing data or projecting future trends exist. These range from the presentation of simple frequency distributions and graphs, to cross-tabulations of two or three variables, to multivariate statistical analyses, such as multiple regression, log linear analysis, and path analysis, to modeling techniques for forecasting time-series data. The different analyses may be easily computed by the use of packaged computer programs.

No matter what particular techniques are selected, two basic questions should be addressed in the analysis: how many and what kinds of families are affected by the policy or program(s) of interest and what policy or program components affect which family structures and/or functions in what matter.

Findings pertaining to the specific impacts of different policy components on family structures and/or functioning can be summarized in worksheet fashion. Figure 15-1 illustrates a sample format for assessing family impacts. As indicated in the step 5 columns, the relationship between a particular policy component and family factors can be categorized in terms of the likelihood that there will be an impact, how strong the impact will be, and what family factors will be affected, such as the families' ability to perform provider, socialization-nurturant, membership, and resource-manipulation functions or the families' general level of functioning.

Step 6: Evaluate the Findings and
Prepare Policy Recommendations

FIA involves two distinct processes: the identification of impacts and an evaluation of the impacts. Whereas steps 1-5 have presented alternative methodologies for identifying and obtaining information to answer the questions of how many and what kinds of families are affected by a particular policy or program and in what ways, the sixth step addresses issues concerning the evaluation of the validity of the findings, the evaluation of the desirability of the findings, and the presentation of policy recommendations.

In the first kind of evaluation, theoretical and methodological deficiencies of the study are reviewed to determine whether the family impacts found or not found can really be attributed to the policy under study or if they might actually be caused by some external factors not considered in the analysis. All research methodologies have some limitations, but in general, results found in carefully designed and executed studies (statistically manipulated or experimentally designed studies that consider multiple interactions between policy components and family outcome over time) can be more readily accepted as representative of the true impact. The second kind of evaluation assesses the desirability of the outcomes. In order to evaluate impacts on this dimension, it is necessary to identify criteria for assessing the desirability of policy-related family impacts—that is, what impacts are considered positive, neutral, or negative.

For impacts that have explicitly stated criteria of desirability, the next substep is to compare the advantages and disadvantages of alternative policies and programs in terms of those criteria. However, criteria of desirability are not always established by clear-cut processes. It is important to recognize the values and assumptions implicit in designating one impact

Policy (Briefly describe):

Implementation component(s)[a]:

Family Impacts[b]	Step 5: Assessment of Impacts					Step 6: Evaluation		
	Is Impact Likely		Magnitude of Impact		Direction of Impact	Desirability		
	Yes	No	Strong	Weak	(indicate)	+	0	−
I. *Structure* Health-social statuses								

II. *Functions*
   Provider
   Socialization
   Family membership
   Resource manipulation								

III. *Functioning*
   Family division of labor
   Quality of interaction								

V. *Other impacts*								

Summary: This policy affects families' ability to

           These impacts are considered

[a]Indicate general policy and policy components(s) under analysis. Individual worksheets can be used for each policy or policy component.
[b]Assess and evaluate familial impacts by filling in proper response in space provided. Individual worksheets can be used for different family types.

Figure 15-1. Assessment and Evaluation of Policy Impact on Families

as more desirable than the other. Clearly some impacts, such as those that put a stress on the family's ability to maintain provider, socialization, and resource-manipulation functions, are undesirable. There is less consensus on the meaning attributed to certain family types and functioning styles.

Once one has assessed policy impacts and, when possible, evaluated their desirability for different population groups, the last step is to summarize the findings and prepare policy recommendations for consideration. This summary should include a catalog of policy impacts on different kinds of families and for different members within the same family. The kinds of policy recommendations the family-impact analyst will make depend on the type and magnitude of policy impacts; an assessment of the validity and reliability of the findings; the analyst's own values and assumptions about desirable family outcomes; and a recognition of the constraints of the sociopolitical environment in which the policy is operating.

Summary

The step-by-step framework for FIA has been successfully utilized to report family-impact studies in the area of child-welfare services, the criminal-justice system, and economic and labor policies (Ory and Leik 1978). Other recent family-policy research has been reported in a special issue of *Journal of Marriage and Family* (Nye and McDonald 1979).

Whether there should be an explicit national family policy or family policies is a question of much debate (Nye and McDonald 1979). Similarly there has been some concern about the role of FIA. Given the conceptual and methodological state of the art of FIA, as well as the plurality of values involved in assessing family impact, it seems premature to mandate FIA as a necessary prerequisite to all policies and programs, as environmental-impact analysis now is. Rather FIA should be viewed as a perspective to sensitize policy makers and administrators to the intended and unintended consequences of public policies and programs on family life.

References

Family Impact Seminar. 1978. *Interim Report of the Family Impact Seminar*. Washington, D.C.: George Washington University, Institute for Educational Leadership.

Guttentag, M., and Struening, E. 1975. *Handbook of Evaluation Research*. Beverly Hills: Sage Publications.

Kammerman, S., and Kahn, A. 1976. "Explorations in Family Policy." *Social Work* 21 (May):181-186.

McDonald, G. 1978. "Family Policy Research and Family Impact Analysis: Implications for Public Policy." Paper presented to the Annual Meeting of the Society for the Study of Social Problems, San Francisco, Calif.

Mattessich, P. 1977. *Family Impact Analysis*. St. Paul, Minn.: State Planning Agency.

_____ . 1979. "Published Sources of Statistics on the Family." *Journal of Marriage and the Family* 41 (August):659-662.

Nye, F., and McDonald, G. 1979. "Special Issue: Family Policy." *Journal of Marriage and the Family* 41 (August).

Ory, M., and Leik, R. 1978. *Policy and the American Family: A Manual for Family Impact Analysis*. Family Impact Series Report. Minneapolis: Minnesota Family Study Center, University of Minnesota.

Rossi, P., and Wright, S. 1977. "Evaluation Research: An Assessment of Theory, Practice and Politics." *Evaluation Quarterly* 1 (February):5-52.

Suchman, E. 1967. *Evaluation Research: Principles and Practice in Public Service and Social Action Programs*. New York: Russell Sage Foundation.

Ukeles, J. 1977. "Policy Analysis: Myth or Reality." *Public Administration Review* 3 (May-June):223-227.

U.S. Congress. Senate. Subcommittee on Children and Youth. 1974. *Hearings: American Families: Trends and Pressures*. 93d Cong., 2d sess.

Vlachos, E., et al. 1975. *Social Impact Assessment: An Overview*. Fort Belvoir, Va.: U.S. Army Engineer Institute for Water Resources.

Wilson, L., and McDonald, G. 1977. "Family Impact Analysis and the Family Policy Advocate: The Process of Analysis." Family Impact Series Report. Minneapolis: Minnesota Family Study Center, University of Minnesota.

Wolf, C. 1976. "Social Impact Assessment: The State of the Art Restated." *Sociological Practice* 1 (Spring):56-68.

16 Assessing Local Policy Impact

A. Lorri Manasse

This chapter describes the development, initial application, and evaluation of an analytical framework for assessing the impact of public-policy experiments. The framework, developed as an integral part of the Los Angeles Unified School District's Community Centered Classroom Program (Tri-C), was designed to overcome many of the common problems of policy evaluation and impact analysis and to produce appropriate and timely data for both decision makers and program managers. The focus here is on the utility of the analytical framework, not on the particular example, although references to the Tri-C application describe and illustrate that utility.

Background

Early in 1975 the Los Angeles Board of Education established a pilot program of storefront schools to serve students who had been formally expelled from the school district. This decision represented a marked departure from previous policy because it implied, for the first time, an assumption on the part of the district of responsibility for the education and rehabilitation of these pupils. Formerly their supervision and rehabilitation had been left to other agencies. However, as the number of expulsions rose rapidly in the early 1970s, reaching several hundred a year by 1974, there was increasing public pressure on the school district to provide services for this client group. Expulsion benefited neither the youngsters, who were often left with no educational opportunity and no structured daytime activities or supervision, nor the community, which bore the cost of additional crime and violence.

The policy also legitimized an alternative approach to education outside the regular school campus, with higher costs and lower than average pupil-to-teacher ratios, and allowed considerable leeway in administrative procedures, curriculum design, and teaching approaches. Tri-C was conceived as a short-term, intensive program to provide educational reinforcement, counseling, and special services. Initial implementation involved seven off-campus classrooms located in leased facilities in the community. Each classroom had a maximum enrollment of ten pupils (grades 7 to 12), with a teacher and two part-time educational aides. Three program counselors provided individual, group, and family counseling, referral to appropriate

161

community agencies, and job development. Later nursing services and health education were added. Students attended class for a minimum day (8 A.M. to 12:30 P.M.), supplemented by an individualized program of extended day activities including work experience, counseling, recreation, community exploration, tutoring, fine arts, and community service.

Given the experimental nature of the program, the shift in policy it represented, the cost to the school district, and the considerable public interest, the importance of developing sound impact indicators was clear. At the same time, all of the problems that often impede policy evaluation and impact analysis were present. For example, there were no resources available for full-time or outside evaluators. Program staff were asked to participate in data collection, a task that imposed extra burdens on their time and energy. In order to prevent program personnel from feeling threatened by the evaluation or from feeling that the evaluation requirements were diverting valuable resources from service delivery and interfering with program effectiveness, it was important that they fully understood the purpose and design of the evaluation component.

The rapidity with which the policy was implemented and the constant changes in program design and program inputs in the early stages of implementation made traditional experimental designs inappropriate. The policy decision had not specified any details regarding the type of program to be provided, and an early administrative decision encouraged flexibility and variety in the seven developing sites. This lack of a stable state is typical today of situations of public learning (Schon 1971) because the essence of experiment—holding some variables constant while manipulating others—is impossible. Any intervention affects more than one variable, and no move has only its intended consequences. The problem is not that information does not exist. On the contrary, situations of public learning contain more information than can be assimilated because they display multiple, complex interactions of variables to which no relatively simple, highly predictive theory is adequate. What is needed, according to Schon (1971) and others (Weiss and Rein 1972; Suchman 1970), is an alternative to the experimental approach that can document the implementation process, specify program inputs, and emphasize case history and systems analysis to generate and test knowledge.

Still another factor complicating the development of impact indicators was the fact that the Tri-C policy decision reflected a number of issues, events, and external pressures on the decision makers. There were multiple goals for the policy and some conflicting values behind the policy. This situation is not unusual, according to Dror (1970), who believes that the educational policy-formation process is largely determined by value judgments and environmental influences. There are frequent internal inconsistencies among educational goals, deriving from a generally unclear vision of the purpose of education, from the vulnerability of educational policy to environmental pressures (which causes education to acquire new goals even while established "old" goals are still accepted), and from the tendency of different groups, both without and within the system, to hold different goals. Goal inconsistency generates the problems of ordering goals, of evaluating them, and of meeting the cost of achieving them. This leads to difficulty in identifying the appropriate data or indicators for impact analysis. Types of indicators appropriate to each goal may differ. Decision makers are interested in outcomes, while practitioners and managers need process data. Furthermore at least four components of a policy system are affected by a policy: the clients (those who receive a service), the implementors (those who provide a service), the decision makers (those responsible for defining problems and providing direction to the system), and the system itself. Different data are appropriate to assess each type of impact.

Analytic Framework

It was necessary to provide data to decision makers that were both valid and timely, in spite of the usual dichotomy between usefulness and validity in evaluation research (Roos 1973). The analytic framework developed for the Tri-C program was designed to:

1. Recognize and account for the political, environmental, and organizational influences on the policy and the latent functions of the policy.
2. Recognize the differing values and data needs among policy makers, managers, and technicians.
3. Accommodate changes in the policy system.
4. Describe the implementation process and specify inputs.
5. Provide feedback to program managers and develop an ongoing self-evaluation capacity to develop data for monitoring, identifying problems, and making incremental changes.
6. Assess impact, here defined as the capacity of a policy to cause change to those exposed to it (Houston 1972).
7. Be cost-effective.

To accomplish all of these goals, a variety of approaches was used over a three-year period. In the first year and a half, efforts emphasized contextual and organizational analysis, descriptive data about the client population, and process data describing implementation and the development of site models. In the second year the evaluation continued to provide basic descriptive data but also began to develop a number of short-term indicators of client impact. Analysis of process data was also able to yield identifiable program components that both defined the nature of the program and appeared to be variables related to pupil impact. Building upon the work of the first two stages, the third stage began to isolate relevant variables more clearly, to develop behavioral objectives, and to develop long-term impact indicators through follow-up data.

The first year's framework had four components (see table 16-1).

1. A contextual analysis of the external and internal factors influencing the initial policy decision, including identification of values, expectations, and, where possible, evaluation criteria. This analysis identified areas of conflict and ambiguity. The boundaries, constraints, and resources of the program were identified, as were those factors that could affect policy decisions but were beyond the control of program administrators. Attempts were also made to identify the types of information that decision makers would find useful for future policy decisions.

2. An organizational analysis of the relationships within the program, the relationships between this program and other subsystems of the organization, and relationships between this program and external systems. Through this analysis values of the various actors were identified in order to consider conflicts in priorities, different perceptions of goals, and influence on outcomes.

3. Documentation and dramaturgic analysis of the policy in operation. This included a comparison between the stated policy and the policy (and program) in operation, identification of shifts in program goals or focus, identification of major problems and issues that were emerging, and descriptions of processes and actors. Dramaturgic analysis differs from contextual and organizational analysis in that it is not an analytical tool designed to identify a particular set of factors involved in the policy process or a particular area of impact. Rather it provides a format for organizing information during the course of program implementation and operation so that emerging patterns can be identified.

4. A description of the program as a whole and a case-study examination of each of the seven sites, based upon the data developed by the staff through its ongoing self-evaluation. Although an outside evaluator helped compile and analyze these data, the data were generated through management of internal data systems and were reviewed by staff at various stages during the program's operation in order to guide them in making operating decisions and modifications.

Application of the Framework

All of the data were collected by program personnel in the regular course of program activity through a variety of instruments, most of them built into

Table 16-1
TRI-C Evaluation Framework

Approach	Primary Activities	Output
Contextual analysis	Historical research Narrative description of decision process Identification of relevant systems, groups, individuals	Definition of basic boundaries, resources, constraints Identification of internal and external influence, potential consequences, potential spillovers of program Explication of values, underlying assumptions of relevant systems and decision makers Identification of data needs
Dramaturgic analysis	Recording and documenting of major meetings, problems, decisions, etc. Preparation of narrative descriptive analysis using dramaturgic approach	Listing of major issues, conflicts, problems to emerge Identification of primary and secondary actors, their values, perspective, self-interested motivations Description of policy in action Comparison of values of decision makers, administrators, teachers
Organizational analysis	Development of organizational chart showing all relationships of program to other elements of system Recording and analyzing activities in terms of meeting conflicting system demands	Identification of values, perspectives, expectations of various system components with regard to program Identification of areas of conflict Specification of program priorities Specification of data needs from program to other components of system Framework for assessing impact of policy on system
Self-evaluation	Compiling client demographic data Interviewing students, parents, staff Recording site activities Recording pupil attendance Recording anecdotal comments on student behavior, attitude Recording student academic activities Preparing weekly reports Logging all referrals, agency contacts Preparing pupil progress reports	Data to decision makers on number of target population served Preliminary data on impact of program on target population Demographic characteristics of population served Impact data on staff Identification of variables; development of projective models for future testing Descriptive data on program inputs Recommendations for modification in policy or program

regular program activities. Documentation included agenda and notes of all meetings, frequent memorandums and progress reports, daily site logs, interview data on pupils and their families, and statistical data on site population and demographic characteristics. The need for careful documentation and continuing evaluation was quickly communicated to the staff. Because staff members recognized that they were to have a role in planning and developing the program and that their efforts could have an impact on future policies, they were more amenable to the concept of evaluation. The importance of providing feedback to decision makers was stressed constantly. The experimental nature of the program and considerable public interest also stimulated staff members to be self-conscious of their activities. In general, staff recognized the need for accurate and complete record keeping and documentation. Involvement of staff members in developing procedures helped them to understand the reasons for certain data needs. Their awareness of the experimental status of the program and the need to prove its efficacy also encouraged their participation. Finally, demonstration that reports were read and data were used made the paperwork less onerous.

One of the more significant factors in effecting staff cooperation was the fact that all data collected had a dual purpose: to develop impact indicators for policy decisions and to provide immediate feedback for program staff to use in ongoing decisions. For example, recognizing that participation in Tri-C might influence their own values and that their values and expectations would surely influence the program, staff members filled out questionnaires developed by the program coordinator in anticipation of baseline data needs when the program began. The responses were shared the next day at a staff meeting and used to stimulate discussion of educational philosophies, perceptions of program goals, ideas, and plans.

Three different kinds of data needs, related to three sets of evaluative criteria, were identified. First, the stated policy goal for Tri-C essentially was to make an educational program available to a target population. The implicit criterion related to this goal required data showing the number of pupils offered the program, the number placed, the percentage of the target population served, demographic characteristics, and service demand. Procedures developed included a demographic data form, a disposition form, and a counselor log sheet. Although the stated policy did not go into detail in defining the characteristics of the program to be provided by Tri-C, it was clear that information on program characteristics would be requested. Daily site logs and weekly reports served the multiple purposes of keeping the program coordinator informed, stimulating regular self-assessment on the part of the site staffs, providing resource data, and indicating emerging patterns in program operation. A third aspect of Tri-C on which data were needed was the impact on pupils and their families. Because all pupils and parents had a preplacement interview, an interview protocol was developed that attempted to anticipate baseline information needs. Post interviews were administered by counselors later. Pupil-progress reports, which summarized behavior, attendance, academic achievement, attitude, and individualized programs, were prepared twice each semester and also for board expulsion or reinstatement hearings. Finally, at the end of each semester, staff participated in small-group, unstructured conferences designed to assess the program. Thematic analyses of these conferences indicated major areas of staff concern.

Contextual Analysis

The contextual analysis was designed to identify internal and external influences on policy, underlying values and assumptions related to policy (and conflicts therein), relevant actors, and basic policy goals. An analytical framework was developed based on Easton's (1969) description of the environment of a poilitical system and Dror's (1970) analysis of educational policy making. The framework identifies the possible systems that might affect policy, the particular issues involved, the effect of those issues, the implicit goals and assumptions, and the potential for future influence. The systems as defined in the framework are not mutually exclusive because social and political phenomena rarely have clear-cut boundaries. Table 16-2 illustrates the framework as utilized, with examples from two systems.

The contextual analysis indicated that the majority of factors influencing the Tri-C policy decision were, indeed, external; they included rising juvenile crime, changing ethnicity of school district's population, and philosophical changes regarding the functions of public schools. The primary goal of decision makers was to provide an educational program for expelled pupils, thereby relieving the political pressure from various groups in the community. Thus their primary interest in feedback data was that which showed how many pupils heretofore unprovided for were now being provided educational services.

In conducting the contextual analysis, Dror's conceptualization of three educational subsystems—policy formation, managerial, and implementation—was especially useful in identifying value conflicts, goal conflicts, and latent policy functions. Four potential conflicts emerged: between rehabilitation and punishment; over the cost of the program and allocation of scarce resources; over the primary function of the program; and, at least potentially, between Tri-C and other alternative programs in the school district or in the community. The analysis identified numerous latent political and system functions of the policy, such as board support of the concept of interagency cooperation, board leadership in the community in using a diversion approach, and a functional role for Tri-C in establishing a new operational branch within the school system.

Table 16-2
Contextual Analysis

System	Issue	Implicit or Explicit Assumptions	Implications
Sociological	Movement for alternative schools	Citizen involvement in education No single best educational model	Can be an ally but must not threaten other alternative programs; created receptive environment.
	Rising juvenile crime	Schools reflect social phenomena and cannot solve social problems	Should schools spend money on delinquents? Can school programs be effective?
Economic	State reimbursements	Schools have responsibility to all pupils	
	CETA		If not renewed, will school district be willing and able to support program?
Political	Public pressure from drug busts	Schools should provide educational program and take some responsibility for rehabilitation	Will program continue after immediate political pressure subsides? Program relieves political pressure.
Legal			
Ethical-cultural			
Demographic			
Historical			
Physical			
Organizational			

The results of the contextual analysis were utilized to plan strategies in relation to other groups, to develop the specific data required or expected by various influence groups, and to design the format, timing, and analytical approaches to be applied to the data collected. For example, given the potential conflict between Tri-C and other alternative programs, it was important to develop data describing characteristics of the target population and characteristics of the program operation, clearly showing what was unique about each. The management strategy of encouraging site-level flexibility in program development and service delivery necessitated separate descriptive evaluations of each program site so that different program models could be identified. In essence, then, the contextual analysis served as a prerequisite for the design of the rest of the evaluation.

Organizational Analysis

The organizational analysis described the characteristics of the policy in action, the design of the program and its fit into the overall system, and the specific service delivery system of the program. It identified actors, units and subsystems, their relevant values, expectations and data needs, and their patterns of interaction. The organizational analysis described the immediate Tri-C service delivery system, three other units in the school system having direct links with Tri-C, and three district subsystems having regular contact with the program though not linked formally. Additionally the three subunits of the Tri-C delivery system—management, counselors, and teachers—were examined in relationship to program goals and values.

The organizational analysis had utility for identifying resources and constraints and for providing a framework for identifying, analyzing, and resolving problems. It identified elements of the larger system most likely to be affected by Tri-C, identified demands placed on Tri-C staff by various other subsystems, identified potential conflicts, and helped to identify potential system resources that might be utilized to strengthen the program. A comparison of decision-maker goals with program personnel goals revealed numerous conflicts or ambiguities, such as ambivalence regarding the goal of returning pupils to regular schools, conflict over the kinds of skills necessary for survival in the system, and conflict over the role of Tri-C counselors.

The organizational analysis resulted in numerous recommendations for program modification. Examples of statements generated by this analysis include these:

1. Tri-C counselors were unable to provide adequate site counseling, resource development, and diversion services because they were asked to perform too many different functions and to relate to too many different levels of the system. Redesign of the counseling component, with division of duties and clear assignment of tasks, was essential.
2. Clear two-way feedback channels had to be developed with the Office of Juvenile Court Relations.
3. In addition to having impact on those directly involved in Tri-C, the program appeared to affect the values of various school personnel regarding the need for educational options; area personnel in their recommendations and actions on pupils involved in expulsions; the Office of Juvenile Court Relations in its case-development functions; and the attitudes of some parents of Tri-C pupils, who saw their children involved in positive behavior.

Dramaturgic Analysis

The primary function of the dramaturgic analysis was to organize data relating to specific issues, showing the evolution of a situation, the relevant actors and actions, and the resolution. This analysis provided a technique for focusing on the key issues or events in the program's development. The simple framework is presented in figure 16-1. Major issues identified through this analysis included the role of the counselor, the stance of teachers in relation to pupils' antisocial behavior, the confidentiality and trust between teacher and pupil, conflict over the major focus of the program as affective or cognitive, the role of aides, the degree to which teachers were pupil advocates, and the question of staff accountability. The format was useful both as a self-evaluation tool for resolving problem situations and as an alternative to a simple program narrative at the end of a program cycle.

Self-Evaluation and Site Descriptions

The statistical and site descriptions provided data related to the primary policy objective of providing an educational program for expelled pupils; they described the nature of the population served and the program provided. The data generated from the ongoing self-evaluation instruments provided information on the day-to-day details of the policy in action, describing individual site subsystems and program operation. The site descriptions provided data for preliminary assessment of impact on pupils and on staff in the form of projective models. Each site description contained:

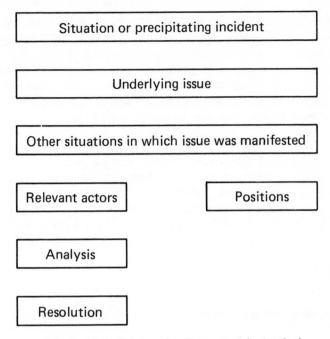

Figure 16-1. Format for Dramaturgic Analysis

1. Demographic information showing the distribution of students by age, sex, ethnicity, and number of children in the family.
2. Teacher attitude toward self, students, discipline, curriculum, and aides.
3. Nature of educational program provided.
4. Changes in student attitudes and feelings, data on attendance, credits earned, rating of teachers, scores on self-acceptance inventory, attitudes toward school, and plans for future.
5. Coded synopses of anecdotal records of site activities and student behavior.

As a result of this analysis, three basic site models could be identified, and a comparison across sites led to projective statements such as the following:

1. Pupils who have jobs or who participate in other meaningful responsible projects (such as tutoring other students) are likely to develop more positive attitudes toward themselves and school and to begin formulating life goals.

2. Tri-C pupils see themselves as victims of the school and of society. Most do not know how to cope with social institutions and authority figures.

3. A certain amount of group recreational activity is conducive to developing group cohesiveness, a characteristic that appears to be related to pupil attendance. Individualized instruction is most effective when it is integrated into an overall group setting.

A preliminary impact statement was prefaced in this way: "Tri-C appears to have had considerable impact on pupils, staff, and others. It is not yet possible to make definitive statements because individual sites varied in program and population, and the total number of cases is small." A list of preliminary impact statements followed, such as: "By the end of the semester, two-thirds of Tri-C pupils had more positive attitudes toward school"; "There is a relationship between students' having personal goals and their attitude toward school"; and "The older the Tri-C pupil, the more credit she or he was likely to earn."

Conclusions and Next Steps

The analytical framework was successful on a number of counts. It was able to identify the stated policy goal and to provide appropriate and timely data to decision makers related to that goal. It described the implementation process, program inputs, and emerging program models while allowing for and adjusting to organizational and policy changes. Preliminary impact statements derived from the analysis were used to guide the development of the second year's framework. This framework continued to provide basic descriptive data and also refined the analysis by developing a number of impact indicators such as pupil attendance, credits earned, parent and pupil attitudes, and pupil self-concept. An analysis of process data yielded a set of identifiable program components that both defined the nature of Tri-C and appeared to be variables related to pupil impact. Such an analysis was possible at this stage, since program inputs had begun to stabilize. The list included:

1. The development of a "family feeling" at each site.
2. Regular, structured group counseling at each site and the use of groups to resolve individual and site problems as they arise.
3. Close and regular contact with the other significant adults in Tri-C students' lives.
4. An academic approach that combines group instruction and group activities with individualized instruction and follow-up to group activities.

5. Structured exposure to environments, cultures, and situations outside the students' previous experience.
6. A team approach on the part of the staff.

Work was also begun during the second year to develop follow-up data to assess long-range impact.

This long-term analysis became the focus of the third year's work. Several hundred former Tri-C pupils were located and their progress tracked. A shift was also made in the third year away from process data and toward outcome data, using three prespecified outcome measures. This shift indicates the evolution of Tri-C from experiment to established program.

A number of factors contributed to the utility and effectiveness of the analytical framework. First, and probably most important, were early administrative decisions to adopt an attitude of "experimental administration" (Campbell 1969) to support flexibility at the implementation level and to use the evolution of different program models as a natural experiment. Corollary to this experimental attitude was an early commitment to developing internal data systems that would provide ongoing process data for immediate feedback, as well as quantitative data to meet the demands of policy makers. Early involvement of program staff in designing data-collection processes and instruments encouraged staff also to adopt an experimental attitude and to see evaluation activities as useful for program improvement rather than as threatening. Staff defensiveness was further reduced by the fact that no particular model was touted as the correct or best approach.

Equally important in the effectiveness of this analytic framework was the early recognition of the political nature of the policy decision and the clear explication of values leading to that decision, goals for the policy, and data needs related to those goals. The two most significant implications of this case study may be the importance of incorporating values into impact analysis and the identification of the importance of system attributes in affecting outcomes. The study illustrates the importance of clearly describing and defining program inputs at various levels and stages of program development so that later analysis can relate outcomes to inputs. Finally the ability to produce early data for decision makers that described program implementation, as well as preliminary impact data for further testing, and the continued refinement of impact data as the program developed and matured, were important factors in the continued support of the Tri-C Program.

References

Campbell, Donald. 1969. "Reforms as Experiments." *American Psychologist* 24:409-429

Costello, Timothy. 1970. "Psychological Aspects: The Soft Side of Policy Formation." *Policy Sciences* 1:161-168.

Dror, Rachel Elboim. 1970. "Some Characteristics of the Educational Policy Formation System." *Policy Sciences* 1:231-253.

Easton, David. 1969. "The Flow Characteristics of Policymaking." In *Policies, Decisions, and Organizations*. Edited by Fremont J. Lyden, George A. Shipman, and Morton Kroll. New York:Appleton-Century-Crofts.

Guba, Egon G. 1975. "Problems in Utilizing the Results of Educational Evaluation." *Journal of Research and Development in Education* 8:114-123.

Houston, Tom R., Jr. 1972. "The Behavioral Sciences Impact-Effectiveness Model." In *Evaluating Social Programs*, edited by Peter H. Rossi and Walter Williams. New York: Seminar Press.

Roos, Noralou P. 1973. "Evaluation, Quasi-Experimentation, and Public Policy." In *Quasi-Experimental Approaches*, edited by James A. Caporaso and Leslie L. Roos, Jr. Evanston:Northwestern University Press.

Schon, Donald A. 1971. *Beyond the Stable State*. New York:W.W. Norton.

Schuman, Edward A. 1970. "Action for What? A Critique of Evaluation Research." In *Evaluating Action Programs*, edited by Carol Weiss. Boston:Allyn and Bacon.

Weiss, Robert S., and Rein, Martin. 1972. "The Evaluation of Broad-Aim Programs: Difficulties in Experimental Design and an Alternative." In *Evaluating Action Programs*, edited by Carol Weiss. Boston:Allyn and Bacon.

Part V
The Role of the
Social Scientist

In this last part, we shift our attention from analysis of the impact to the analyst, the social scientists performing the impact analysis. Two complementary discussions of the social scientist's role in impact analysis comprise this part. Drawing on experience in an interdisciplinary energy-research project, Steven Ballard, Allyn Brosz, and Larry Parker discuss four roles—linking policy research and the academic community—that they find essential in their research. John Foster then focuses on one role model, that of the advocate, in which he argues that we should depart from the presumption that policy issues are purely technical problems and should take into account the self-interest involved in policy analytical work. Both chapters consider questions of feasibility and the role of competing values.

17 Social Science and Social Policy: Roles of the Applied Researcher

Steven C. Ballard,
Allyn R. Brosz, and
Larry B. Parker

Research on policy impact increasingly has focused on the practical application of research (Cook and Scioli 1975, pp. 3-8; Lindblom and Cohen 1979). Causes of this trend include demands for relevancy in social-science research, the gradual development of the policy sciences, and increased needs in the policy-making community for better information about the impacts of public policies (Kochen 1975; Galbraith 1967). This increasing emphasis on applied-policy research has focused more attention on strategies for the successful application of social science to social problems. Several strategies have helped to increase the potential use of our research while maintaining linkages to the academic community.

Approach

Three general themes have characterized our approach to applied-policy analysis. The first is early involvement. To be successful, utilization activities can never be an afterthought. Although these activities may increase over the course of a project, particularly as reports are completed, relationships with government agencies, parties at interest, and other users must begin at the research design stage if the research is to be utilized. The second theme is continuing relationships. The research team conscientiously maintains user relationships throughout the course of the project. Thus while early involvement is critical for establishing awareness of and interest in the project, contacts and participation must be continuous in order for the research team to establish and maintain the trust and credibility necessary for the successful utilization of research projects. The third is scientific credibility. While applied researchers must pay attention to approaches for increasing utilization, they also must maintain credibility in the scientific

This chapter is based largely on research being performed by the Science and Public Policy Program, University of Oklahoma, for the U.S. Environmental Protection Agency under contract number 68-01-1916. The authors would like to acknowledge the contribution and support of other members of the research team, particularly Irvin L. White, Don E. Kash, and Michael D. Devine. The authors are solely responsible for the content of this chapter.

research community, an often-neglected but critical component of applied-policy research. Academic credibility facilitates the application of current social-science knowledge—including theories, methods, and data bases—to social problems. Social-science knowledge often is available and applicable, and the capability of researchers to draw on this knowledge is important to the overall quality of the applied-research product (White, Ballard, and Hall 1978).

In contrast to many nonacademic and profit-making policy-research groups, university-based applied-policy research is judged by scientific as well as practical criteria. Contract research proposals at the federal level frequently are evaluated by social scientists. Applied-research products also are typically subject to thorough technical reviews. This may occur directly—for example, because the researcher explicitly submits the product to the scientific community (in both university positions and private research organizations) through the peer review process—or indirectly—for example, when research findings threaten particular organizational or political interests, in which case discrediting the findings by attacking the scientific validity of the study may be easier than addressing the substance of the proposal.

Multiple Roles of the Social Scientist

These general approaches and philosophies suggest multiple roles for social scientists in applied policy research, particularly those of the social scientist as substantive expert, information processor, change agent, and disciplinary scholar. The discussion that follows is based largely on our experience in an applied interdisciplinary research project, "Energy from the West," in which the likely effects of energy development in the western United States were identified and alternative policies for dealing with these impacts were analyzed.

Substantive Expert

Public-policy problems are almost always difficult. Existing literature is seldom sufficient or is too fragmented to provide a clear, unambiguous problem definition. Conditioning factors, such as relevant social and political variables, are frequently unknown or rapidly changing. Uncertainty about the information that does exist often generates disagreement rather than consensus about the nature of problems and their solutions. As a result, there seldom exists a single analytical approach through which one can capture a problem's complexity and deal with its uncertainties.

Every problem area identified as being significant to the development of western energy resources can be so characterized, but perhaps the best example is water availability in the Colorado River Basin. Although the quantity of water existing in the Colorado River Basin, the amount currently unused, and the amount available for future uses have been analyzed extensively, little agreement exists about these data or their implications (White et al. 1979). More importantly, such estimates represent only part of the total water-availability picture. The data can be influenced significantly by unresolved political conflicts, such as the quantities of water belonging to native Americans and/or needed to protect the environment.

Researchers dealing with these uncertainties must become substantive experts. This is not meant to suggest that they lose sight of analytical or theoretical tools, which are obviously important to the research. However, as a first step in learning which tools and approaches are appropriate, social scientists need to become familiar with the policy system that influences the particular problem at hand. In this effort, the analysts need to address several general matters. These include knowledge of competing definitions of a problem, its historical development, relevant legal and institutional factors affecting its development, the people and groups influenced by the problem, and social and economic implications (White, Ballard, and Hall 1978). For example, the analysis of water availability in the Colorado River requires knowledge of such factors as the historical values of water use in the West, various interstate and international compacts and agreements, the legal complexities of state appropriation systems, Bureau of Reclamation policies and pricing strategies, the interests and behavior of various native American and environmental interest groups, and water needs for future energy development.

Knowledge of these factors will not resolve the uncertainties associated with estimating current water supplies or the possibility of future shortages. However, it does provide a starting point for further analysis and in effect serves as a filter through which various theories, analytical approaches, and data bases can be passed, and increases as well the likelihood that the ultimate product will provide relevant information.

Information Processor

Information production—the generation of original knowledge—is usually the primary role of scientific researchers and is an activity highly rewarded within academe. Equally important in applied research is information processing: selecting, integrating, and synthesizing existing knowledge about particular problems, impacts, and policy alternatives. Integrating knowledge helps to provide a better understanding of research needs, including some that are not evident at the outset of the project.

This form of knowledge is not synonymous with literature review but entails a broader task, deriving from the fact that problems can be, and usually have been, studied in a wide range of disciplines. Thus it is necessary to apply knowledge from a variety of perspectives to the particular problem at hand and thereby integrate these knowledge bases into one coherent picture. For example, the availability of water supplies for energy development in the Colorado River has been approached from engineering, hydrological, economic, historical, and political perspectives (Mann 1978; White 1975; Stockton and Jacoby 1976).

Disciplinary Scholar

The scholarly activities of applied researchers are difficult to achieve and controversial because they typically require trade-offs between science and utility. Applied research operates within time, information, and resource constraints that often make theory construction and thorough analysis difficult. Indeed some critics argue that these trade-offs cannot be made (Feldman 1976, pp. 19-27).

Coleman (1972), among others, presents the problems of the scholarly minded applied researcher as a dichotomy between policy-making and scholarly environments: the world of the academic discipline versus the world of policy and action. The goal of discipline-oriented research is an increment to existing knowledge in a substantive area, the development and analysis of theoretical insights. Policy or applied research, according to Coleman, is "decision oriented," intended both to serve as a guide for action and to bridge the two worlds.

The distinction between discipline and policy research distorts our conception of the research process because these two worlds are more complex and interrelated than Coleman acknowledges. It is probably more accurate to view applied research as a logical extension and/or counterpart of discipline research in which the researcher becomes a scholar-practitioner. (Although the relationship between applied and basic research typically is viewed as a sequence, with basic knowledge being the prerequisite, it is a mistake to view this as a necessary condition. For example, theories of magnetism followed rather than preceded the development of the compass. See Böhme 1977.) Formal training in an advanced-degree program exposes researchers to the theoretical literature and analytical procedures of the discipline. This work provides a base for undertaking applied-policy research much as basic research in the natural sciences provides a pool of knowledge that can be used to develop new technologies and solve problems. Subsequently researchers might choose to combine disciplinary knowledge and policy experience. Jones (1976) suggests that this is academic-based research with policy effects.

Communication between basic and applied environments is important because it improves the research product and feeds relevant research findings back to appropriate disciplines. In this regard, the researcher as scholar-practitioner appears to be ideally situated to bring disciplinary knowledge to bear on the research process and to communicate with academic and research audiences throughout.

Several communication strategies can be pursued to increase the impact of applied-policy research on disciplinary knowledge. Results of research can be presented at professional meetings and in scholarly journals, and social scientists can be utilized in outside review processes to add to analytical and substantive expertise. Groups of social scientists can also be used as technical advisory committees, and they can conduct workshops to review and help design various aspects of policy analysis. These communication mechanisms do more than add to expertise; they also serve as a check on the overrepresentation of the perspectives and values of the research team or of any particular institution (Kash 1977).

Our study has also used substantive and theoretical knowledge from political science and attempted to develop new insights. Substantively political-science literature has helped us to understand political institutions, public decision processes, and problem and issue categories that are affected by the development of energy resources. Although public-policy problems do not usually coincide with disciplinary boundaries, disciplinary knowledge can increase our understanding of their causes and impacts. In the case of water availability for energy development in the western United States, political-science literature was useful in developing the team's knowledge of the administrative and regulatory setting, public-involvement processes, and the importance of intergovernmental relations in water-resource policy making.

The study has also used and developed theoretical knowledge. For example, since intergovernmental relationships are critical to problem categories such as water availability and to the overall political and social context within which energy resources will be developed, it was important for the research team to understand the dominant themes in intergovernmental and particularly state-federal relations. In that regard, work done by Jones (1976) and Lieber (1975) improved our understanding of intergovernmental relationships, particularly regarding centrally directed federalism applied to environmental policy. As our knowledge about the western region and the effect of energy-resource development on the region increased, we revised and expanded this theoretical understanding (Hall, White, and Ballard 1978) in an attempt to keep our work relevant to both society and the profession of political science.

Change Agent

At the same time that information is being produced and processed, the applied researcher can also become a change agent—an actor who helps decide how the information is used to change a particular problem or the way the problem is characterized. Disagreement exists regarding whether or how actively researchers should pursue this role and how certain important ethical questions that become apparent should be resolved. With many researchers still seeing themselves in the role of "speaking truth to power" (see Weiss 1977, pp. 1-23), this role is critical to whether and how social research is used ultimately.

The general tasks of the change agent are to develop strategies for communicating and disseminating information to users. Among the various mechanisms developed in our own research to establish early involvement and to promote continuing relationships with users, one of the most important has been an advisory committee composed of a range of public and private interests affected by problems associated with western energy development. In addition to representativeness, the primary requirements for successful use of the advisory committee are early and frequent involvement. Our advisory committee was formed a few months after the project started, and the committee continued both to advise on the purpose and scope of the project and to review the research products throughout its three years. Input from the advisory committee was viewed as an integral part of the design of the project.

A second change-agent strategy is to distribute reports widely. To enhance awareness of the project, a report, *Draft Policy Analysis Report*, was distributed to approximately five hundred parties at interest both regionally and nationally; the same range of interests represented in the advisory committee was included among those receiving the publication. The report was also distributed to various scientific and research audiences for their reaction to and comments on the technical quality of the information and to learn about other approaches to the research.

The form of dissemination activities—specifically the packaging of research products and presentation of findings to the most directly affected audiences—is crucial. While it is necessary to produce and disseminate detailed supporting documents for the subject matter covered by this study, summary documents that are short and nontechnical and use graphics, maps, charts, and other visual presentation techniques are also quite useful.

A third strategy is personal interaction. In a broad sense, personal interaction begins with the research team's learning about the system: the people, activities, and institutions that influence the variety of problem areas affected by resource development. Corresponding to this learning process, the team gradually interacts with the system by visiting development sites and affected areas, attending conferences and workshops on energy- and environment-related topics, and establishing oral and written contact with other participants in the system.

Closely related to personal interaction and also critical to utilization are presentation strategies; these are important throughout the project. For example, about midway through the project, the team presented its preliminary findings to several federal agencies, state and local government officials, industry and civic groups, and other interested parties. These dissemination activities typically consisted of a slide presentation focused toward the specific audience. Technical and political problems and issues likely to occur in Wyoming, for example, will be somewhat different from those in southern Utah, and the presentation reflected this different orientation.

In the change-agent process, researchers must be sensitive to the ethical questions raised. Among the more important ethical questions raised by those strategies are these:

1. Control of the research agenda: User involvement and responsiveness to immediate information needs almost certainly will mean a loss of some control over the research agenda.
2. Organizational resistance: The incorporation of user perspectives early in the research can lead to pressures to change or omit findings that are potentially damaging to the particular interests of affected organizations.
3. Pathology of trust: Establishing trust with the user community is perhaps the key to utilization; yet if the researcher is successful, research products of any quality may be accepted by the user.
4. Misused information: Information may not be used, it may be incorrectly used, or only parts of it may be used to legitimate a decision already made.

A few general perspectives on each of these questions have emerged from our experience. These problems establish a creative tension in applied research. If the researcher's goal is to maximize the chances for information utilization, then these kinds of problems appear to be a logical result. Creating a balance among these issues is one of the challenges of applied research.

Social-science research inherently is governed by some set of values (Weiss 1977), and conflicts over values are to be expected in both applied and basic research (Sjoberg 1975). Values and value conflicts can affect the choice of topic, alternatives examined, methods, and theory. However, social scientists have seldom incorporated values into their research methodology, even though they have generally become more sensitive to value conflicts in recent years (Sjoberg 1975).

The participatory mechanisms discussed here place considerable responsibility upon researchers for controlling information development and enhancing the utilization processes. Along with this responsibility, these mechanisms provide a means by which values and value conflicts can be recognized. For example, submitting draft reports for critical review by both scientific and policy communities provides feedback on the technical quality and the values and interests of important stakeholders. The success of this strategy depends on the diversity of outside participants and the research team's willingness to include relevant participants at the earliest possible stages of research. For example, generally we distributed draft papers well before we as individual authors and as a team were satisfied with them. Although this procedure is contrary to commonly held scientific norms, it facilitates participation because reviewers can contribute their views before problems and issues or alternative policies become rigidly defined.

Although the team does risk some credibility in the short term by this procedure, long-term problems generally have been avoided by the research team's willingness to include reviewers' perspectives and to continue to upgrade the quality of the report. Early distribution has also been useful to the team's capacity to understand the diverse and often complex values affected in a given substantive problem area. The effort to establish credibility through continuing relationships with both the scientific and policy communities helps the research team to understand and represent a broad range of values and reduces the risks of misuse of the research products.

The benefits of performing this balancing act can be substantial. The need for credible, timely, and usable information is significant, as has been particularly evident in recent energy policy. However, applied researchers must also realize that regardless of how well the research is performed, information may not be used in the manner they prefer. There is little to support the contention that good quality research will be used and bad quality research will not be, either theoretically in terms of how innovations are adopted (Rogers 1962) or empirically (Berg et al. 1978). Whether research is used depends on a variety of factors, including political legitimation (Aaron 1978), interpersonal relationships (Patton 1978), and the attention given by the researchers to increasing the utilization potential (House and Jones 1977).

Conclusion

The utilization of applied research requires the interplay of several factors, many of which are beyond the control of researchers. However, utilization potential can be enhanced by several strategies that link the researchers to the policy-making community, while maintaining scientific credibility. These strategies must be pursued as an early and continuing aspect of applied research. This kind of activity presents several difficulties, including the ambiguity associated with the absence of a single analytical approach directly applicable to the problem, dual accountability to scientific and policy communities, and ethical questions related to the active involvement of researchers in the change process. However, the multiple roles suggested here also establish a creativity in the research process and, in our experience, greatly improve the potential utility of the research.

References

Aaron, Henry. 1978. *Politics and the Professors: The Great Society in Perspective*. Washington, D.C.: Brookings Institution.

Berg, Mark R., et al. 1978. *Factors Affecting Utilization of Technology Assessment in Policy-making*. Ann Arbor: University of Michigan, Institute for Social Research.

Böhme, Gernot. 1977. "Models for the Development of Science." In Ina Spiegel-Rösing and Derek de Solla Price, eds., *Science, Technology, and Society*. Beverly Hills: Sage Publications.

Coleman, James S. 1972. *Policy Research in the Social Sciences*. Morristown, N.J.: General Learning Press.

Cook, Thomas J., and Scioli, Frank P., Jr. 1975. "The Interaction of Substance and Method in the Study of Public Policy." In Frank P. Scioli, Jr., and Thomas J. Cook, eds. *Methodologies for Analyzing Public Policies*, pp. 3-8. Lexington, Mass.: Lexington Books, D.C. Heath and Co.

Feldman, Elliot J. 1976. "An Antidote for Apology, Service, and Witchcraft in Policy Analysis." In Phillip M. Gregg, ed., *Problems of Theory in Policy Analysis*, pp. 19-27. Lexington, Mass.: Lexington Books, D.C. Heath and Co.

Galbraith, John Kenneth. 1967. *The New Industrial State*. New York: New American Library.

Hall, Timothy A.; White, Irvin L.; and Ballard, Steven C. 1978. "Western States and National Energy Policy: The New States Rights." *American Behavioral Scientist* 22:191-212.

House, Peter W., and Jones, David W. 1977. *Getting It Off the Shelf: A Methodology for Implementing Federal Research*. Boulder, Colo.: Westview Press.

Jones, Charles O. 1976. "Policy Analysis: Academic Utility for Practical Rhetoric." *Policy Studies Journal* 4:281-286.

Kash, Don E. 1977. "Observations on Interdisciplinary Studies and Government Roles." In Richard A. Scribner and Rosemary A. Chalk, eds., *Adapting Science to Social Needs*, pp. 147-178. Washington, D.C.: American Association for the Advancement of Science.

Kochen, Manfred, ed. 1975. *Information for Action: From Knowledge to Wisdom*. New York: Academic Press.

Lieber, Harvey. 1975. *Federalism and Clean Waters: The 1972 Water Pollution Control Act*. Lexington, Mass.: Lexington Books, D.C. Heath and Co.

Lindblom, Charles E., and Cohen, David K. 1979. *Useable Knowledge: Social Science and Social Problem Solving*. New Haven: Yale University Press.

Mann, Dean E. 1978. "Water Planning in the Upper Basin of the Colorado River." *American Behavioral Scientist* 22:213-236.

Patton, Michael Quinn. 1978. *Utilization-Focused Evaluation*. Beverly Hills: Sage Publications.

Rogers, Everett. 1962. *Diffusion of Innovations*. New York: Free Press.

Sjoberg, Gideon. 1975. "Politics, Ethics, and Evaluation Research." In E.L. Struening and M. Guttentag, eds., *Handbook of Evaluation Research*. Beverly Hills: Sage Publications.

Stockton, Charles W., and Jacoby, Gordon C., Jr. 1976. *Long-term Surface Water Supply and Streamflow Trends in the Upper Colorado River Basin*. Lake Powell Research Project Bulletin Number 18. Los Angeles: University of California, Institute of Geophysics and Planetary Physics.

Weiss, Carol. 1977. Introduction to Carol Weiss, ed., *Using Social Research for Public Policy Making*. Lexington, Mass.: Lexington Books, D.C. Heath and Co.

White, Irvin L.; Ballard, Steven C.; and Hall, Timothy A. 1978. "Technology Assessment as an Energy Policy Tool." *Policy Studies Journal* 7:76-83.

White, Irvin L., et al. (1979). *Energy from the West: Policy Analysis Report*. Washington, D.C.: Environmental Protection Agency.

White, Michael D. 1975. "Problems Under State Water Laws: Changes in Existing Water Rights." *Natural Resources Lawyer* 8:359-376.

18 An Advocate Role Model for Policy Analysis

John L. Foster

Many proposals to increase the level of information and rationality in public policy making emphasize the development of a profession of policy analysts who are familiar with various research tools, the substance of specific policy areas, and the politics of the policy-making process (Bell 1967; Dror 1967, 1968, 1971; Horowitz and Katz 1975; Lasswell 1951, 1970; MacRae 1975; but see Lazarsfeld 1975). Nevertheless, most accounts of the use of policy-evaluation efforts suggest a very minimal impact on the policy-making process (Goldstein et al. 1978; Rein and White 1977; Wholey et al. 1970; Weiss 1977). One possible explanation for this apparent lack of evaluation utilization is the role of the evaluator in the policy-analysis process.

Some Policy-Analysis Role Models

The most common role models for applied research are variations of what Rein and White (1977, pp. 130-136) label the "problem-solving" approach. Goldstein et al. (1978, p. 36) summarize the underlying assumptions of this approach by noting that most evaluation research arises from "an intellectual climate which assumes most social programs as well as their solutions are merely 'technical problems' which will respond to the manipulations of a professional." One version of the problem-solving perspective is roughly analogous to the medical professional's role model. Policy goals or priorities are assumed to be rather clear or obvious, and the professional is presumed most qualified to determine the probable impact of various programs or proposed options. Policy making then becomes a matter of closely following professional recommendations.

A slightly different variation of the problem-solving theme resembles an engineering approach. This perspective assumes that a client's goals and priorities may be somewhat unclear or conflicting but that professional analysts are qualified to determine the impact of programs and the likely results of proposals. These assumptions make it reasonable to utilize an evaluator to describe the impact of existing programs or to determine the consequences of a series of options, while final decisions are reserved for traditional political processes.

A number of well-known conditions, however, seem to limit the use of these problem-solving approaches in a number of public-policy-making situations (Goldstein et al. 1978; Rein and White 1977; Weiss 1970, 1972, 1973; Wildavsky 1969). Policy evaluation is expensive, time-consuming, and often hampered by a lack of clearly defined policy goals. Often program administrators are less than totally cooperative during the evaluation process. Many officials are either unable to understand evaluation reports and/or politically unwilling to utilize them. Furthermore some evaluators themselves may lack technical competence or are restricted from using appropriate research designs by pragmatic considerations. These obstacles have led several observers to prepare lists of suggestions for evaluators who do not wish to have their work go unutilized (Enthoven 1975; Weiss 1972, chaps. 1, 2, 6; Weiss 1973; Wholey et al. 1970, chap. 7).

At least two additional role models for policy analysis seem to have evolved. Both suggest that evaluation may have a greater and different impact than suggested in the problem-solving-model critiques. For example, some recent research suggests that policy evaluation has a diffuse, long-term impact on policy making that both scholars and practitioners often miss. Caplan (1977) and Weiss (1977) both find that policy evaluations can affect decision makers' problem conceptualizations, perceptions of policy priorities, and sense of basic causal relationships. This process over time can help "to shift the agenda and change the formulation of issues" (Weiss 1977, p. 535) in a particular field and thus affect policy. Weiss labels this the "enlightenment" effect.

The enlightenment effect obviously is difficult to document. The causes of long-term social patterns are particularly hard to isolate, and the general problem is complicated in this instance by decision makers' frequent inability to remember the source of particular ideas or interpretations. Furthermore many scholars and consultants may not even consider the possibility of the enlightenment effect because the problem-solving model is the dominant paradigm. However, the enlightenment interpretation is intuitively appealing. The belief that educational facilities have little impact on educational quality has been common since the Coleman Report (Coleman et al. 1966), and many have felt that Project Headstart has little lasting effect since the Westinghouse-Ohio University study appeared.

An analyst intentionally playing the enlightenment role can suggest alternate conceptualizations, interpretations, or value premises to a client. The analyst may also conduct preliminary, speculative quantitative analysis of causal relationships in a field but is always aware of goal conflicts in public policy, limitations of quantitative techniques, and the political constraints on evaluation usage. The analyst will not expect his or her work to have an immediate impact on policy but will be pleased if some long-term changes eventually can be traced to this work. Of course, this is not likely to be a particularly appealing approach for most consultants or academicians oriented toward activism. It also does not seem to describe the present conduct of a significant amount of policy analysis.

A third interpretation of the role of the analyst is the advocate model of policy analysis, which seems to have evolved with even less attention than has the enlightenment model. The primary task of the advocacy analyst is to provide the best possible case for a client's policy recommendation or continuing program rather than to seek a detached, objective answer for the question of whether the program works. This style seems most likely, and perhaps most desirable, when two conditions are met. The first is reasonably clear client commitment to a program or policy option. The second is relatively high uncertainty about the impact of the program on other parties and on society in general. In these instances, analysts are often sought to argue a causal link between the program (or option) and the generally desired results and to deemphasize any conflicting values that may appear to follow. Thus analysis essentially becomes a form of ammunition and legitimacy to be utilized in the policy process.

The policy process, in turn, can become somewhat analogous to the legal process. That is, it essentially becomes a conflict in which two or more competing parties' claims are represented by professional advocates who make the strongest possible case for their clients. The forum for these conflicts can be any sector of the polity: legislatures, legislative committees, regulatory commissions, agency staff meetings, courts, as well as the general public. Kourilsky (1973) and Levine (1973) suggest a version in which specific decision makers formally appoint two or more competing adversary analysts to ensure that various perspectives are represented and considered. However, the process that seems to have evolved generally seems much more informal and much less controlled than their portrayal of it.

One favorite example of the evolving advocacy-analysis approach occurred during 1971 congressional hearings of the nutritional value of several breakfast cereals. Some analysts for consumer groups claimed that the nutritional value of many cereals and their cardboard packaging were approximately equivalent. Analysts for the cereal industry rejoined that the consumer advocates had distorted matters by evaluating the cereal in isolation rather than as a portion of a complete breakfast. Most products apparently did provide a substantial percentage of daily requirements when combined with milk and fruit. Nevertheless, most manufacturers have subsequently increased the nutritional level of their products with additives, which suggests that policy change can stem from an advocacy conflict.

Perhaps a great deal of present policy analysis resembles this advocacy style much more than it resembles either the problem-solving or enlightenment models. Edwards and Sharkansky (1978, p. 129) observe that the "common expression at the Defense Intelligence Agency is that it exists to provide justification for what Operations (the action arm of the military) wants to do." Jones (1977, p. 177) notes that "one might do well to assume that evaluation is primarily an exercise in justification." Caplan (1977, p. 72) classified 20 percent of his sample of high federal officials as "advocacy users" because their "use of social science information is limited, but when used, its use is almost exclusively dictated by extra scientific forces to the extent that they will at times intentionally ignore valid information that does not fit the prevailing political climate." Finally such classic discussions of information in the policy-making process as Lindblom's (1968, pp. 65-66) "partisan analysis" and Wildavsky's (1969) "Rescuing Policy Analysis from PPBS" essentially suggest an advocacy alternative to traditional approaches.

Advocacy-Analysis Model

The major implications of the advocacy-analysis approach do not appear to have been considered carefully, although concern with an advocacy role model is common in fields such as planning and journalism, and Lasswell (1970) did suggest the advocate analogy for some portions of the policy-evaluation process.

The apparent spread of advocacy analysis appears rather easy to explain and somewhat inevitable. Advocacy analysis is consistent with the axiom that people do not often act contrary to their perceived self-interest. Problem-solving analysis may be useful when client and evaluator agree on goals, but if this agreement does not exist, clients may find themselves in a position where they are (or perceive they are) asked to pay (with money, access, and cooperation) for information that can be used against their perceived self-interests. The advocacy analyst, in contrast, is almost always viewed as an ally and is thus much more likely to be employed and utilized. This, in turn, leads to a series of questions on how best to deal with advocacy analysis.

Credibility

One such question concerns credibility. Would the policy-analysis profession have greater credibility if it openly acknowledged the advocacy role? Much of the appeal of problem-solving analysis is the appearance of objectivity detached from self-interest. Yet if this detachment is unlikely and a subtle, implicit form of advocacy analysis inevitably is developing and perhaps dominating the field, then the most critical question is not whether advocacy analysis will destroy the profession's credibility but whether the policy-analysis profession will have greater credibility and influence if it acknowledges its tendencies to advocate rather than trying to cover them.

Wilensky (1964) makes several interesting observations relevant to this question. He notes (p. 138) that groups aspiring to professional status must convince potential clients that they have mastered a body of knowledge necessary to perform services for the clients that the clients cannot master as quickly for themselves and can be trusted to perform these services in the best interests of the clients and refrain from the inevitable opportunities to exploit client vulnerability. A group does not achieve true professional status by making implausible claims of either technical competence or professional ethics. Hence, the legal profession, based on acknowledged advocacy, has been accorded professional status for centuries, while groups such as real estate and insurance agents whose advocacy is thinly disguised have not been.

Desirability

A similar issue is the general desirability of an overt advocate model. A likely first reaction to the question of whether society will benefit if advocacy analysts come to dominate is a resounding "no." Problem-solving ideals and the search for truth are well established in the academic and scientific communities where the policy-analysis movement originated, and advocacy analysis initially appears to be a complete perversion of these ideals. On the other hand, advocacy analysis is one way to introduce some information into the policy process. And a series of competing advocates given an opportunity to cross-examine could potentially contribute a great deal toward more informed decisions.

Advocacy analysis fits rather well with the well-known pluralist descriptions of the American political process, which raises several additional disquieting questions. What would that process do to poorly organized interests in society? How does it affect the conservative status-quo tendencies in public decision making? Policy analysis is not cheap; hence well-organized and -funded groups would seem to be the most likely clients. Furthermore the inability to form groups around collective interests discussed by Olson (1965) is well known. Thus there would seem to be a natural tendency for advocacy analysis to follow the legal pattern of the greatest talent being hired by the groups that are already well represented, which would reinforce biases toward the status quo.

If there is some degree of inevitability in the development of advocacy analysis, however, we might better ask whether to acknowledge it rather than whether to allow it. Perhaps an open admission of the tendency toward advocacy in applied research, and the possibility of such persons becoming most accessible to well-established interests, could lead to a form of public-defender analyst supported by government and private interests to represent both poorly financed groups and the frequently unorganized collective interest. The present number of public defenders and legal-assistance societies may be the result of clear, acknowledged evidence of imbalance in the distribution of legal professionals.

Training

Another concern if advocacy analysis is evolving is the appropriate professional training. Present policy-analysis preparation, dominated by the problem-solving paradigm, is a blend of formal academic work and on-the-job training (Lasswell 1970). Most formal academic courses in public policy cover analytical techniques and research design, the policy process, and the substance of policies in various areas. Courses that treat the role of evaluation in the political process and the role of the evaluator are relatively rare (Foster 1978). That portion of the evaluator's training usually is left to on-the-job training, which likely confronts the aspiring analyst with situations in which the problem-solving-oriented university training is either misleading or irrelevant. A major consequence of this may be a great deal of cynicism and perhaps sweeping rejection of research techniques and design in particular and university training in general.

Future policy-analysis training should attempt to address this problem. Course work can be designed to introduce students to various policy-analysis roles before they implicitly internalize one role during job experiences. It seems particularly important for students to develop an ability to recognize the variations between roles and to identify the role most appropriate to a particular circumstance.

Ethics

Course work in the analyses of roles also should introduce variations in ethical standards between problem solving and advocacy forms of evaluation. The general ethical principle of advocacy analysis becomes maximum service to a client rather than the traditional search for truth. However, if we are to control the advocacy-analysis tendencies, it is important for students to recognize that this shift in goals does not imply a rejection of all of the principles of conventional academic inquiry. Advocacy analysis can have ethical limits. For example, service to a client does not necessarily condone outright fraud such as the creation of fictitious data, or attempts to present totally misleading impressions, or conscious destruction of crucial evidence. At the same time it does not ask an analyst to refrain either from data presentations that place a client's arguments in the most favorable light or from emphasizing interpretations most favorable to a client in situations where data are consistent with multiple interpretations.

Summary

The advocacy model of policy evaluation, considered here as an alternative to the traditional problem-solving model and the more recently recognized enlightenment model, is not necessarily the superior approach in either an ideal sense or even in all actual policy-making situations. The advocacy approach to evaluation also will not resolve a number of basic hurdles to rational decision making such as the expense, time, and technical competence required for evaluation; the tendency for evaluators to focus on the impact of new rather than well-established programs; and the inability to determine actual program goals. However, an advocacy model appears to be a much more forthright approach to a growing reality. Furthermore the eventual result of its use might be considerably more information on policy impact being introduced into the political process, which could, in Wildavsky's words (1969, p. 190), provide "a higher quality debate and perhaps eventually public choice among better known alternatives."

References

Bell, Daniel. 1967. "Notes on the Post Industrial Society, Parts I and II." *Public Interest* 6:24-35, 7:102-118.

Caplan, Nathan. 1977. "Social Research and National Policy." In Stuart Nagel, ed., *Policy Studies Review Annual*, 1:68-75. Beverly Hills: Sage Publications.

Coleman, James S., et al. 1966. *Equality of Educational Opportunity*. Washington, D.C.: U.S. Government Printing Office.

Dror, Yehezkel. 1967. "Policy Analysis: A New Professional Role in Government Service." *Public Administration Review* 27:197-203.

_____. 1968. *Public Policy Making Reexamined*. Scranton, Penn.: Chandler.

_____. 1971. *Design for Policy Sciences*. New York: Elsevier.

Edwards, George C., and Sharkansky, Ira. 1978. *The Policy Predicament*: *Making and Implementing Public Policy*. San Francisco: W.H. Freeman.

Enthoven, Alain. 1975. "Ten Practical Principles for Policy and Program Analysis." In Richard Zeckhauser et al., eds., *Benefit Cost and Policy Analysis*, pp. 456-465. Chicago: Aldine.

Foster, John. 1978. "The Politics of Policy Analysis." In William Coplin, ed., *Teaching Policy Studies*. Lexington, Mass.: Lexington Books, D.C. Heath and Co.

Goldstein, Michael, et al. 1978. "The Nonutilization of Evaluation Research." *Pacific Sociological Review* 21:21-43.

Jones, Charles O. 1977. *An Introduction to the Study of Public Policy*. 2d ed. North Scituate, Mass.: Duxbury Press.

Horowitz, Irving, and Katz, James. 1975. *Social Science and Public Policy in the United States*. New York: Praeger.

Kourilsky, Marilyn. 1973. "An Adversary Model for Educational Evaluations." *Evaluation Comment* 4:3-8.

Lasswell, Harold. 1951. "The Policy Orientation." In Daniel Lerner and Harold Lasswell, eds., *The Policy Sciences*, pp. 3-15. Palo Alto: Stanford University Press.

_____ . 1970. "The Emerging Conception of the Policy Sciences." *Policy Sciences* 1:3-14.

Lazarsfeld, Paul. 1975. "The Policy Science Movement: An Outsider's View." *Policy Sciences* 6:211-222.

Levine, Murray. 1973. "Scientific Method and the Adversary Model: Some Preliminary Suggestions." *Evaluation Comment* 4:1-3.

Lindblom, Charles. 1968. *The Policy Making Process*. Englewood Cliffs, N.J.: Prentice-Hall.

MacRae, Duncan. 1975. "Policy Analysis as an Applied Social Science Discipline." *Administration and Society* 6:363-388.

Olson, Mancur. 1965. *The Logic of Collective Action: Public Goods and the Theory of Groups*, Cambridge, Mass.: Harvard University Press.

Rein, Martin, and White, Sheldon. 1977. "Can Policy Research Help Policy?" *Public Interest* 49:119-136.

Weiss, Carol. 1970. "The Politicization of Evaluation Research." *Journal of Social Issues* 26:57-68.

_____ . 1972. *Evaluation Research: Methods for Assessing Program Effectiveness*. Englewood Cliffs, N.J.: Prentice-Hall.

_____ . 1973. "Where Politics and Evaluation Meet." *Evaluation* 1:37-45.

_____ . 1977. "Research for Policy's Sake: The Enlightenment Function of Social Research." *Policy Analysis* 3:531-545.

Wildavsky, Aaron. 1969. "Rescuing Policy Analysis from PPBS." *Public Administration Review* 29:189-202.

Wilensky, Harold. 1964. "The Professionalization of Everyone?" *American Journal of Sociology* 70:137-158.

Wholey, Joseph, et al. 1970. *Federal Evaluation Policy*. Washington, D.C.: Urban Institute.

Index

Index

About the Contributors

Steven C. Ballard is assistant professor of political science and assistant director of the Science and Public Policy Program, University of Oklahoma. His research has been on applied policy analysis, and he has published articles on knowledge utilization, technology assessment, social indicators, intergovernmental relations, and energy policy.

Edmund Beard is associate professor and chair of the Department of Political Science at the University of Massachusetts, Boston. He is the author of *Developing the ICBM: A Study in Bureacratic Politics* and *Congressional Ethics: The View from the House*, as well as articles on conflict of interest in the executive branch, presidential nominating politics, and the politics of urban revitalization in Boston.

Allyn R. Brosz is assistant professor of political science at Virginia Polytechnic Institute and State University, with research interest in the uses, impacts, and control of science and technology. His current research includes an analysis of federal policy for commercializing new energy and environmental technologies. He has coauthored several research reports for the Environmental Protection Agency and the Office of Technology Assessment.

Marshall Carter, currently an officer in the Foreign Service, was an associate professor of political science at Ohio University. She has published other materials on borders and law enforcement based on research begun while she was a visiting professor at the University of Texas, El Paso. Her other publications include articles on the Nigerian judicial process and two coauthored texts, *American Government: A Brief Introduction* and *The World of Politics.*

M. Margaret Conway, associate professor of government and politics at the University of Maryland, has research interests in electoral politics, the role of the mass media in political socialization, and economic regulation.

Fred S. Coombs is an associate professor in the Department of Educational Policy Studies at the University of Illinois at Urbana-Champaign and director of the Office for the Analysis of State Education Systems at that institution. He is the author of numerous articles on educational reform and the politics of French education, and is coauthor of *Introduction to Governance in Education.*

Gillian Dean is an assistant professor of political science at Vanderbilt University, currently on leave at the Brookings Institution. Her research on American domestic social policy includes work on organizational factors affecting implementation and evaluation and on policy impacts.

Peter DiToro is employed as a bilingual admissions specialist for the Boston Housing Authority and is enrolled in the Massachusetts Institute of Technology's graduate program in urban studies and planning.

John L. Foster is an associate professor of political science and director of the Master of Public Affairs Program at Southern Illinois University at Carbondale. His research interests are the impact of information upon and occurrence of innovation in the decision-making process, bureaucratic rigidity, and simulation.

Phyllis Strong Green is assistant professor of political science in the Department of Human Ecology and Social Sciences, Cook College, Rutgers University.

Richard J. Hardy is an assistant professor at the University of Missouri, where he teaches courses on state public policies, policy analysis, and American politics. He has published several articles on the impact of the Civil Rights Act of 1964, on the incomes of blacks and women, and on the policy impact of reapportionment.

William E. Hudson is assistant professor of political science and director of the Public Administration Program at Providence College. Currently he is doing research on the impact of federal policy on local government budgeting.

E. Terrence Jones is professor of political science and director of the Public Policy Administration Program at the University of Missouri-St. Louis. He is the author of *Conducting Political Research* and numerous articles on urban politics, public policy, and research methods.

A. Lorri Manasse is a research associate in the Program on Educational Policy and Organization of the National Institute of Education. She also teaches at the Washington Public Affairs Center of the University of Southern California. Formerly she developed and directed the Community Centered Classroom Program for the Los Angeles Unified School District. She received the doctorate in urban studies from the University of Southern California. Her current research interests include community organization, citizen participation, policy evaluation, and organizational innovation.

Lester W. Milbrath is director of the Environmental Studies Center and professor of political science at the State University of New York at Buffalo. His recent research has emphasized the study of environmental beliefs, perceptions, attitudes, and values. He also does research on "paradigm shift" and quality of life. He is the author of *The Washington Lobbyist* and *Political Participation* and editor of *The Politics of Environmental Policy*.

Harold Molineu is an associate professor of political science at Ohio University, specializing in international relations and American foreign policy. He has also served as director of parliamentary relations for the North Atlantic Assembly in Brussels. His most recent research and publications have been in U.S. human-rights policy, with particular reference to the Helsinki Agreement.

Kathryn E. Newcomer is an assistant professor at the University of Nebraska, where she teaches regulatory policy making, policy analysis, political behavior, and American politics. She has published articles on congressional voting behavior, the diffusion of public policies, and the policy impact of reapportionment.

Marcia G. Ory is assistant professor in the Department of Public Health at the University of Alabama Medical Center. Her chapter is based on her experiences as a postdoctoral fellow in the family-impact analysis of health-care policies and programs at the Minnesota Family Study Center, University of Minnesota, 1977-1978. Her current interests are an examination of the impact of chronic illness on patients and their families and the development and testing of health education–behavioral strategies for health-promotion maintenance.

Larry B. Parker is a graduate research assistant with the Science and Public Policy Program, University of Oklahoma, and a doctoral candidate in political science. His research has been in applied-policy analysis, with special emphasis on technology assessment, energy policy, and knowledge utilization.

Nicholas C. Peroff is associate professor of public administration at the L.P. Cookingham Institute for Public Affairs and associate dean of the School of Administration of the University of Missouri-Kansas City. He received the Ph.D. degree from the University of Wisconsin, Madison. His teaching and research interests are in public-policy analysis, urban administration, and urban planning. He has contributed a number of articles to professional journals and is the author of *Menominee: A Study of Indian Policy in the United States* (forthcoming).

Debra W. Stewart is associate professor of political science at North Carolina State University. She has published articles in *Public Administration Review*, *Publius*, and *Public Personnel Administration: Policies and Practices* and has consulted widely on affirmative action in governmental systems.

Ronald J. Terchek is associate professor of government and politics at the University of Maryland and specializes in democratic theory, political participation, and modern political theory. He is the author of *The Making of the Test Ban Treaty* and coeditor of *Foreign Policy as Public Policy* (forthcoming). He has also published articles in *Political Science Quarterly*, *Journal of Peace Research*, *Psychoanalytical Quarterly*, and other journals and has contributed chapters to various books.

About the Editors

John G. Grumm is professor of government at Wesleyan University in Connecticut and teaches public policy, American state politics, and legislative systems. He is the author of numerous articles and monographs on policy analysis and comparative legislative behavior.

Stephen L. Wasby is professor of political science in the Graduate School of Public Affairs at the State University of New York at Albany. His research and writing have focused on the federal courts, particularly the Supreme Court. He is the author of several books, including *The Impact of the United States Supreme Court* and *The Supreme Court in the Federal Judicial System*, and he edited a Policy Studies Organization volume, *Civil Liberties: Policy and Policy-Making*. He is a member of the editorial boards of *American Politics Quarterly*, *Justice System Journal*, and *Policy Studies Journal*.